THE ATTACK ON NOVA SCOTIA SCHOOLS

The story behind 25 years
of tumultuous change

Grant Frost

Formac Publishing Company Limited
Halifax

As always, to K, without whom, nothing is possible.

Copyright © 2020 by Grant Frost

All rights reserved. No part of this book may be reproduced or transmitted in any form or by any means, electronic or mechanical, including photocopying, or by any information storage or retrieval system, without permission in writing from the publisher.

Formac Publishing Company Limited recognizes the support of the Province of Nova Scotia through the Department of Communities, Culture and Heritage. We are pleased to work in partnership with the Province of Nova Scotia to develop and promote our cultural resources for all Nova Scotians. We acknowledge the support of the Canada Council for the Arts, which last year invested $153 million to bring the arts to Canadians throughout the country. This project has been made possible in part by the Government of Canada.

Cover design: Tyler Cleroux
Cover images: THE CANADIAN PRESS/Andrew Vaughan

Library and Archives Canada Cataloguing in Publication

Title: Attack on Nova Scotia's schools : the story behind 25 years of tumultuous change / Grant Frost.

Names: Frost, Grant, 1968- author.
Description: Includes bibliographical references and index.
Identifiers: Canadiana (print) 20190047801 | Canadiana (ebook) 2019004781X | ISBN 9781459505759 (softcover) | ISBN 9781459505766 (EPUB)
Subjects: LCSH: Education—Nova Scotia. | LCSH: Educational change—Nova Scotia. | LCSH: School management and organization—Nova Scotia. | LCSH: Education and state—Nova Scotia.
Classification: LCC LC2891.N6 F76 2019 | DDC 379.716—dc23

Formac Publishing Company Limited
5502 Atlantic Street
Halifax, NS, Canada
B3H 1G4
www.formac.ca

Printed and bound in Canada.

Advance Praise for
The Attack on Nova Scotia Schools

"Making sense of the politics of education here in Nova Scotia has become a lot easier since I read this book."
— Robert Devet, Editor, *Nova Scotia Advocate*

"A fabulous exposé."
— Sheldon MacLeod, Host, *The Sheldon MacLeod Show*

"Everyone interested in public education should read this book. The final chapter strikes a powerful note of hope."
— Alan Joyce, Nova Scotia Parents for Public Education

"Grant Frost's research provides the legwork to understand how political, social and economic shifts have continually shaped the Nova Scotia education system, chipping away slowly over time, to come to our uncertain present."
— Pamela Rogers, Researcher and Policy Analyst, Canadian Teachers' Federation

"A thoughtful and comprehensive account of how the global education reform movement was imposed on Nova Scotia."
— Erika Shaker, Education Program Director, Canadian Centre for Policy Alternatives

Contents

List of Acronyms	6
Foreword	7
Introduction	10
CHAPTER 1: The Roots of Educational Reform	15
CHAPTER 2: Inventing the Myth that Our Schools Are Failing (1980–2000)	23
CHAPTER 3: The Global Education Reform Movement (2000–2010)	38
CHAPTER 4: Connecting Education and Employability (1990–2010)	49
CHAPTER 5: The Think Tank Campaign to Privatize	70
CHAPTER 6: How the Media Turned Nova Scotia Against Its Teachers (2010–2014)	85
CHAPTER 7: The Political Response: The Minister's *Action Plan* (2014–2015)	104
CHAPTER 8: A Clash of Agendas: The Teacher Job Action (2016–2017)	118
CHAPTER 9: The Glaze Report: Control and Power to the Province (2017–2019)	135
CHAPTER 10: How Can We Defend Public Education in Nova Scotia?	153
Acknowledgements	162
References	163
Index	177

List of Acronyms

APEF — Atlantic Provinces Education Foundation
AIMS — Atlantic Institute for Market Studies
AP — Advanced Placement
BEA — Black Educators Association
BLAC — Black Learning Advisor Committee
CCPA — Canadian Centre for Policy Alternatives
CMEC — Council of Ministers of Education, Canada
EGLs — Essential Graduation Learnings
FUD — Fear, Uncertainty and Doubt
GERM — Global Education Reform Movement
HRSB — Halifax Regional School Board
IB — International Baccalaureate
KIPP — Knowledge Is Power Program
MIT — Massachusetts Institute of Technology
MLA — Member of the Legislative Assembly
NDP — New Democratic Party
NCLB — No Child Left Behind
NPE — Network for Public Education
NSTU — Nova Scotia Teachers Union
NSTSO — Nova Scotia Teachers Speaking Out (Facebook page)
OECD — Organisation for Economic Co-operation and Development
O_2 — Options and Opportunities
PISA — Programme for International Student Assessment
PCAP — Pan-Canadian Assessment Program
RAND — Research and Development (US global think tank)
SAC — School Advisory Council
TPA — Teachers' Professional Agreement (TPA1, TPA2, TPA3)

Foreword

I have been working in education for the better part of twenty-five years. In that time I have taught in a wide variety of settings, ranging from working in isolated First Nations communities in northern Saskatchewan to working with troubled, inner-city youth in Halifax, Nova Scotia. I have taught a wide spectrum of subjects to a wide array of students and have organized everything from lunch-hour clubs to high-school musicals and beyond. I have written provincial curricula, developed provincial standardized tests and facilitated provincial professional development days. I have witnessed students accomplish amazing and wonderful things, and I have attended more of their funerals than I thought my heart could bear. I have dealt with parents who were angry, parents who were scared, parents who were immensely proud of their kids and parents who were disappointed. I have spent the equivalent of about a dozen years attending post-secondary institutions to gain additional degrees and diplomas. In short, I am a pretty average Nova Scotia school teacher.

About six years ago, though, I was reading Nova Scotia's provincial paper of record, *The Chronicle Herald*, when I came across an op-ed piece written by someone who I later found out had close ties to the Atlantic Institute for Market Studies (AIMS), Dr. Paul W. Bennett. Bennett's piece made me so angry that I decided to send in a rebuttal to the newspaper, which, much to my surprise, the editorial desk decided to publish.

Since that time, I have written well over a quarter of a million words about education, having commented on every manner of practice, policy and procedure on my blog Frostededucation.com, and as a contributing writer for *The Chronicle Herald*. I have also, with no small modicum of luck, held several positions with my local teachers' union, positions that have seen me take a unique and often personal role in government–labour relations in Nova Scotia over the past few years. This has included, most recently, being elected as a local union president for Halifax County in 2016, and running, unsuccessfully, for the Nova Scotia Teachers Union (NSTU) provincial presidency in 2018.

I point this out not to be self-aggrandizing, but to provide some background experiential context. From about 2012, I was as engaged as any teacher could be in the events that were unfolding, educationally speaking, in our province. And although I had a sense something was awry, I couldn't put my finger on the reason why things were developing the way they were. I would read a piece of often poorly researched commentary about how our public education system in Nova Scotia was failing and marvel at how the same piece would be published simultaneously in another province's paper, criticizing that system for the exact same reasons. I would read a position paper, full of errors and obvious omissions, and then see the same inaccurate statements repeated across multiple and supposedly reputable media outlets. I would hear unsupportable solutions offered to complex educational problems, with little evidence provided to demonstrate a connection between the two, and then sit back and watch in indignation as the source of those solutions was interviewed on the six o'clock news.

At the time, I was not able to see the forest for the trees. It wasn't until I began the research for this book that distinct patterns began to emerge. As I compiled my research and spoke with authors and experts such as Diane Ravitch and Pasi Sahlberg, I realized that I was not imagining the connections. The events taking place in Nova Scotia were indeed part of a much larger trend, a trend that most of us missed, even though it was happening right under our noses.

It should surprise no one that the views you are about to read are heavily influenced by my own personal bias, as much as they are informed by the small role I played in the events of 2015–18. And although I always stand by the words I have put to paper, I make no claims at being an authority or an expert. I am a public-school teacher and union activist who wants to share his experience and views with parents and citizens who are interested in understanding what has unfolded in Nova Scotia's public-education system.

Grant Frost
October 2019, Halifax

Introduction

On Friday, February 17, 2017, something astounding happened in Nova Scotia.

For the first time in over 120 years of educational history, the province's schools were empty because its teachers did not show up for work. Instead, they were part of a large crowd of protestors who had arrived in Halifax to surround Province House twenty people deep. They were joined by concerned parents, students and representatives from many other labour organizations. At issue was the impending passage of Bill 75, which was about to receive final reading and become the *Teachers' Professional Agreement and Classroom Improvements Act*. The *Act* legislated a wage pattern upon the province's teachers and brought an end to the first-of-its-kind job action, undertaken by a group of people who were not particularly well known, in Nova Scotia at least, for their militancy.

This moment marked the apex of what had been a long and difficult struggle against a rising tide of educational reformism that was sweeping the globe and had finally arrived on our relatively isolated shores. This *Act* was presented as being about balanced budgets and fiscal management, and indeed, had it occurred in isolation, that could perhaps have been argued to have been the case. However, Bill 75 was enacted at a time when the fabric of public education worldwide was under assault, at risk of being torn asunder by the forces of globalization, right-wing think tanks and private business interests.

In many respects, Nova Scotia seems like an odd choice of setting for a book that examines the impact of such global trends. We are, after all, a fairly small province of less than a million people. We have around 375 public schools, under the management of eight educational authorities. The day-to-day task of educating the province's 120,000 or so children falls to about 9,300 public-school teachers. All told, when considering some of the other educational behemoths that exist in this country — the Toronto District School Board on its own is easily three times our size — it is easy to see our province as a small fish in a large pond.

Economically speaking we are, as well, a fairly small player. Nova Scotia still relies heavily on natural resources to make ends meet, with our primary exports consisting of the likes of seafood and lumber products. There is little manufacturing to speak of, and although there have been some sparks of innovation, I doubt anyone would classify us as a technological hub. Considering this economic base, it is not surprising that we are also a heavily rural province. In fact, according to at least one source, we are one of Canada's least urban provinces, with 43 per cent of our population living in rural communities.[1] These communities have, much like their counterparts across the country, struggled to stay alive, suffering from the cruel realities of outmigration, an aging population and under-employment. This has been the way of things here for as long as most of us can remember. However, when it comes to post-secondary education, we punch well above our weight. There are nine universities within our ocean-wrapped borders, as well as a number of smaller colleges. We have an impressive array of public community colleges offering a wide variety of both skills-based and academic programs. And, of course, we have privately run educational firms, training schools and institutions. A respectable number of these educational sites are in smaller communities and are major contributors to their local economies.

This presents a very interesting dichotomy for Nova Scotia. On one hand, a sizeable portion of our population struggles with poverty and job security on a daily basis. On the other, it is difficult to throw a rock and not hit an institution that purports, by its very existence, to be able to change that. Education has always sold itself as a way for individuals to improve their lot. Public education has gone further by promoting itself as the great social equalizer.

This promise of realizing greater success through education becomes even more alluring in a have-not province like Nova Scotia. If you wish for a future for your own children free of job insecurity, and you live in an area of low economic prospects, education can be seen as a panacea. Yet, somehow, our economic woes seem almost perpetual. We can ask pointed questions about the capacity of our system to do what many claim is its primary purpose.

That question of ultimate purpose is at the core of so many controversies surrounding public education. What, precisely, are we trying to achieve through our public-education system? Originally, public school was about training factory workers. It wasn't until the twentieth century that the idea of using schools to create a more just and moral society began to take root. There are many (myself included) who have come to believe that the purpose of public education should be defined in a much broader context than simply being a means to a good job. The book *Flip the System*, edited by Jelmer Evers and René Kneyber,[2] argues that this very lack of a common working definition for the purpose of public education has allowed this economic connection to flourish. As we have moved through the latter part of the twentieth century and into the twenty-first, the connection between education and economics has strengthened. Raising up the masses has become not about emancipation, but about vocation. Courses and subjects are valued, not for their capacity to broaden the mind, but for their capacity to broaden employability prospects.

This almost desperate wish for public education to bring our region out of its economic malaise makes it particularly susceptible to what folks in the business world refer to as FUD: Fear, Uncertainty and Doubt. It is a well-known tenet of private-sector marketers that if you can create FUD within a population about either an issue they are facing or a competitor's product, you can advance your own brand. From food to automobiles to the housing market, FUD is one of the most powerful tools in the arsenal of those who wish to separate you from your hard-earned dollars.

Fear, Uncertainty and Doubt works best when the issue or the product in question is of particular value to the consumer. If, for example, I can convince the public that my competition's product is damaging to their health, or better yet, the health of their children, I can position mine as offering a solution. It really doesn't matter, financially at least, if my product is better, or if the original product is damaging. All I need do is convince the public this is the case, and they will flock to my products.

Welcome to the education wars of the twenty-first century.

Current educational reformists preach the gospel of the public-education system universally failing students, often with little evidence on which to base the claim. They have repeated this mantra with mind-numbing tenacity until it has become an accepted premise. This is what I like to call (with a nod to FUD) Unsupported Deficiency Syndrome. Essentially, if you tell people often enough that a publicly funded system, like education, is failing, they come to believe it, even in the face of evidence to the contrary.

Once Unsupported Deficiency Syndrome has been firmly established, reformists begin to promote changes to the status quo, which they frame as fundamentally flawed and often as being protected by self-serving unions. In areas of high unemployment, this tends to be an easy sell. In a province like Nova Scotia, with some of the highest poverty and unemployment rates in the country, it is easy to portray unionized workers as being undeservedly compensated at the expense of the average taxpayer. Pensions, sick days and working conditions all become the target of public ire and a key tool in the reformists' battle chest.

In many ways, Nova Scotia served as almost the perfect petri dish for those who wished to reform education. In the lead up to that fateful February day, and in the months that followed, educational reformism swept across the previously quiet province with a vengeance, feeding on public insecurity and wreaking havoc on the system, as well as on the people who serve within it and the students and parents who rely on it.

In this book, I will offer my explanation of how Nova Scotia arrived at this pivotal moment in its educational history and how ideas based in the practices of big business and the economic theory of neoliberalism came to dominate the dialogue.

CHAPTER 1
The Roots of Educational Reform

The reform agenda for public education has a few key characteristics. They include: increasing accountability measures within the system, increasing focus on core subjects and increasing emphasis on competition, all working together toward the goal of school improvement. We will return to these ideas later, but this summary provides a good frame of reference from which to begin.

Although identifying these key characteristics is relatively simple, it is a much more challenging task to trace their source. This is particularly true in Canada, where we do not have a national education authority. The responsibility for education, outside of Indigenous communities, lies with the provinces, each with the ability to develop their own curriculum and educational approaches. Nationwide, there are as many different systems as there are provincial education departments, which results in little consistency when it comes to the scope and sequence of educational change. One province may wholeheartedly embrace a particular educational thrust, while another may only adopt certain pieces. Sometimes, this trend of "adopt as you will" sees one jurisdiction picking up an educational trend just as another is abandoning it. Nova Scotia's adoption of "discovery math" a few years ago, just as Alberta was moving away from it, is one such example.[1]

The educational reform movement, in Canada and internationally, does, however, sprout from some strikingly common roots. In order to understand the overall picture, we must start with a rather strange and seemingly unrelated theory of economics and a gathering of like-minded individuals in the Swiss village of Mont Pèlerin. There, in 1947, Nobel prize–winning economist Friedrich Hayek brought together some of the most influential thinkers of his time to re-examine and in some sense re-invigorate some classical ideas of *laissez-faire* economics. At the inaugural meeting, Hayek created an entity known as the Mont Pelerin Society, which, over the course of the next several decades, developed what became one of the most formative and influential ideas of the twentieth century and beyond: neoliberalism.[2]

At its core, neoliberal ideology is centred around the theory that market forces are the best way to organize a free society. Allowing free-market forces such as competition and supply and demand to dictate how a society functions is the best way to ensure that it thrives. From the beginning, neoliberalism rejected the idea of the state as a distributor of wealth to the middle class, and instead saw the role of government as only creating the conditions under which free markets could flourish.

Now, just as *educational reform* defies simple definition, *neoliberalism* can be difficult to pin down. For our purposes, however, it is useful to highlight some other key tenets of this ideology.

To start with, neoliberalism is often associated with austerity measures by the state and increased privatization of public services. This is due to the fundamental belief of the neoliberals in market forces. If you have a government-run monopoly of a service, the lack of any outside pressure through competition creates stagnation. Without competition, neoliberals would argue, there is no motivation for change.

Introducing competition and allowing for privatization offers further benefits in that if services are privatized, then efficiencies can be found to reduce costs. If I am running an entity with an essentially unlimited government budget (think: health care), then I am under no particular pressure to reduce spending. However, if the same entity were to be run as a for-profit enterprise, entrepreneurs would compete with each other to find ways to offer the same services at a lower cost.

This "for-profit" model for public services has become the calling card of the neoliberal movement, with the ultimate goal being a reduction in government spending and interference in the markets. If traditional (and costly) government spending areas are privatized, then taxation levels can be reduced. Creating a "pay-for-use" system for services previously provided by governments allows for less money to be controlled by the state and places more wealth in the hands of the private sector, allowing for greater accumulation of individual wealth and greater individual freedom.

Considering that the ultimate end of the neoliberal agenda is the smallest possible role for government and the greatest possible opportunities for the private sector, it is perhaps not surprising that there is a great deal of wealth supporting the idea. One of the challenges neoliberals have faced (and have always complained about) is the amount of influence applied by the middle- and working-class population on democratic governments. Although not impossible, ensuring the appropriate politician is sitting in the appropriate chair in order to ensure market-based policies are adopted can be a challenge even for the wealthiest neoliberal supporter.

What can be effective, however, is utilizing a third-party organization to push the ideology out across the land in a voice resounding with conviction. This allows neoliberal thinking to cross political lines. Instead of the ideas being the platform of a particular party, they become part of the common understanding of how things should work.

Enter the entity known as the think tank.

Think tanks have been an integral part of the neoliberal movement since the creation of the Mont Pelerin Society. In 1949, Hayek wrote an essay entitled "The Intellectuals and Socialism," in which he explored the idea of groups of intellectuals acting as what he called "professional secondhand dealers in ideas."[3] These intellectuals did not need to be original thinkers, nor did they need any particular expertise in the field. They did not need to possess any special knowledge on the subject upon which they were expressing views, nor, Hayek explained, did they even need to be particularly intelligent. They simply needed to be willing to use their station in life to spread an idea, and the rest of us would eventually come to accept their ideas as truth.

Hayek envisioned a wide group of professionals, from artists to writers to radio commentators, working to advance the ideals of neoliberalism without having any overt association with the neoliberal movement itself or specific political-party affiliation. These secondhand dealers would write commentary and produce reports, which, although purporting to be based in objective research, would be heavily biased toward advancing the cause of neoliberalism. These dealers would then speak publicly in defense of the research, to advance the cause of the free-market state.

In his 2014 book *Harperism: How Stephen Harper and His Think Tank Colleagues Have Transformed Canada*, Donald Gutstein provides a wonderfully clear (and somewhat frightening) outline of the massive influence Hayek and his followers have had on the affairs of modern-day Canada.[4] Gutstein draws a clear line of connectivity between the establishment of the first neoliberal think tank, the Institute of Economic Affairs (IEA) in London in 1954, and several contemporary Canadian clones, including the Fraser Institute and the Atlantic Institute for Market Studies (AIMS), an organization that features prominently in later chapters.

Since the time of Hayek, the concept of the think tank has spread across the globe, and the ideas of neoliberalism have proliferated. Supported by wealthy private donors, think tanks have spent decades (and a considerable amount of cash) promoting their ideologies. One of the largest of these is a group known as the Atlas Network, which operates out of Arlington, Virginia. This organization has a network of almost five hundred think tanks in ninety-four countries, all advancing the cause of neoliberalism and free-market economics.[5] In 2016 alone, Atlas gave out over $5 million in various grants to neoliberal organizations, while accepting almost $15 million in donations from private donors.[6]

It would be inaccurate to claim that all think tanks are neoliberal — indeed, there are a number of decidedly left-leaning, more socially minded organizations, including such Canadian entities as the Broadbent Institute and the Canadian Centre for Policy Alternatives. According to Gutstein, however, in Canada alone, neoliberal think tanks out-perform their more socially progressive counterparts by a ratio of seven to one when it comes to media mentions. When looking at the global context and the spread of neoliberalism, just considering the Atlas Network gives one a sense of the pervasiveness of the ideology. With each one of the five hundred think tanks working to advance the cause, and with each one attracting its own funding from donations by similarly minded people (as well as perhaps accessing grants from Atlas), the sheer magnitude of the effort to advance the cause of neoliberalism globally is awe-inspiring.

As one of the key tenets of neoliberalism is the accumulation of personal wealth at the expense of more collective undertakings by governments, it is not surprising that much of the support for these think tanks can be traced back to the world's wealthiest people. The Atlas Network was founded by British millionaire Antony Fisher,[7] who had originally established the IEA, and who was also the co-founder of the Fraser Institute,[8] Canada's most influential neoliberal think tank, in the early 1970s. That organization has been pushing the neoliberal agenda since its inception, and has received financial support from Atlas, as well as from American billionaires,[9] the Koch brothers,[10] and the

Weston family, the owners of Loblaws.[11] According to the Canada Revenue Agency, the Fraser Institute saw total revenues of $11 million in 2017, $5 million of which was received from other charitable groups.[12]

The Fraser Institute, like other think tanks, does not produce any sort of consumable product. It exists solely to promote ideas, in this case the ideas of neoliberalism. To that end, it works tirelessly on spreading the ideology through commissioning research papers, publishing articles and distributing neoliberal op-ed pieces through news networks across the country. According to the organization's own annual report from 2017, this includes having published about 1,400 articles in Canadian dailies and generating over 40,000 mentions across a variety of media platforms.[13]

The Fraser Institute is, like most think tanks, a registered charity. Thus, when people donate to the Fraser Institute, that donation is tax deductible. Considering that neoliberals wish to take money out of the hands of the government, there is no small irony in this. The government is essentially supporting the funding of charitable organizations that, at their very heart, exist to impede that self-same government's ability to fund charitable organizations.

The regional manifestation of the neoliberal think tank in Atlantic Canada was the Atlantic Institute for Market Studies (AIMS) until it was subsumed into the Fraser Institute in November 2019. For more than twenty years, AIMS attempted to influence regional governmental policy supported by local business tycoons. Since its inception, the organization had educational reform as one of its key mandates.

The extent to which AIMS, and its neoliberal messaging, impacted the general public's understanding of any number of issues is, of course, difficult to ascertain. Much like any other organization, AIMS saw peaks and valleys of influence, appearing from time to time to grab the spotlight before fading once again into relative obscurity, at least as far as the general public is concerned. However, one of the many traits that AIMS shared with its larger counterparts was its incessant media presence, which as it turns out, has had a major influence on Nova Scotian educational policy.

There is another rather interesting connection revealed in Gutstein's book between AIMS and the global spread of neoliberalism. The organization was originally established by Brian Lee Crowley in the mid-nineties, thanks in large part to the support of Atlas. Crowley would move on to establish the Macdonald-Laurier Institute, which enjoyed a particularly cozy relationship with the neoliberal Conservative government of Prime Minister Stephen Harper, and has itself become one of the most influential neoliberal think tanks in the nation, rivalling the Fraser Institute. Crowley first came to accept the neoliberal doctrine when he was convinced by Hayek's arguments around the role of government in the markets and was reportedly on record as supporting the efforts of famed neoliberal British Prime Minister Margaret Thatcher to "privatize everything she could."[14]

So, while it may seem odd to be opening a book about the struggles faced by the education system in our small corner of the world with a discussion of major international economic thinking, it is important to see how the two are intertwined. Without Hayek, there would have been no Atlas Network, no Fraser Institute and no AIMS. In the absence of a basic understanding of the pervasiveness of the neoliberal ideology, it is difficult to wrap one's head around the role played by an economic theory in the educational upheaval witnessed in Nova Scotia over the past twenty-five years — upheaval that has impeded contract negotiations, inspired educational reviews, incited province-wide strike action and resulted in the abolition of democratically elected school boards.

With the understanding that the events that have unfolded (and, indeed, continue to unfold) in Nova Scotia are more globally connected than they may first appear, I turn to our story. How is it that an idea, based solely on economic theory, the enhancement of private wealth and a competitive market would come to play such a pivotal role in educational discourse? How did public education, traditionally a collective public activity, become so dominated by what is, at its heart, an individualist ideology?

In what may seem yet another bizarre twist of storytelling, we turn our attention to an unknown Russian technician, a 200-pound satellite and a moment that would change forever the very purpose of public education.

CHAPTER 2
Inventing the Myth that Our Schools Are Failing (1980–2000)

Trying to see a linear progression in educational reform in Canada is problematic, due in part to our system of provincial educational governance. However, much like Levi's and rock 'n' roll, many educational ideas that emerge on the Canadian landscape are imported. The United States has long had a heavy influence on Canadian institutions, and education is no different. From whole language to outcome-based education, many of the trends that have come to our country have originated stateside. Unlike Canada, the US does have a national education authority, and it has, in many instances, driven the educational narrative in both countries.

To pinpoint the exact moment that led to all the tumult in our education system in the past few years, we need to go back to October 4, 1957, at approximately 7:28 pm.[1] It was then that an unknown Russian technician flipped the switch that sent the world's first artificial satellite into the annals of history. Yes, oddly enough, this chapter in our story begins with Sputnik 1.[2]

To understand the implications of the Sputnik launch, we need to understand the America of the time. The US had emerged as a world superpower after the Second World War, and during the euphoric afterglow, the American psyche saw itself as unbeatable. The economy was booming, the country was recovering and everyone was basking in the post-war bustle and hum. In 1955, President Dwight Eisenhower announced to the American people that the country would be launching a satellite into orbit within two years. Not long afterward, the Russians began their own space program, and the infamous Space Race was born.

It was a serious blow to the American ego when Russia launched Sputnik. It didn't matter that the US would later launch their own satellite successfully; they had failed to do it first. In many ways, this moment epitomized and solidified the American cultural expectations around competition. Competition was good, but losing was not an acceptable outcome.

Throughout the tumultuous sixties and seventies, the US continued to struggle with its identity and this notion of national superiority. The Vietnam War left many Americans disillusioned, and as the 1980s dawned, the country was in a state of cultural and economic flux. With the election of Ronald Reagan in 1981, however, American economic policy veered sharply toward the neoliberal philosophy. Many of the policies of "Reaganomics" were neoliberal in nature, including a focus on reducing taxes and increasing free markets. Reagan's now-famous firing of around 11,000 unionized air traffic controllers was very much aligned with the anti-labour stance of the neoliberals.[3] Hayek himself believed unions actually hurt the working class. He decried the idea that unionized labourers might be paid more than non-unionized ones and preferred a model where each worker would negotiate their salary and benefits with their employer on an individual basis.[4]

The application of neoliberal ideas on education systems had first been suggested in 1955 by Hayek contemporary and Mont Pelerin Society member Milton Friedman, who argued that it was high time to critically examine the collective nature of public education.[5] He saw government support of public education as working against the "freedom of the individual, or, more realistically, the family," and argued that if the cost of educating children could be met by "the great bulk of families in a community, it might be both feasible and desirable to require parents to meet the cost directly." With more than a touch of elitism, Friedman further suggested that this move would have an impact on the size of families, particularly reducing those of a lower socio-economic status:

> *It is by no means so fantastic as may at first appear that such a step would noticeably affect the size of families. For example, one explanation of the lower birth rate among higher than among lower socio-economic groups may well be that children are relatively more expensive to the former, thanks in considerable measure to the higher standards of education they maintain and the costs of which they bear.*[6]

As well as suggesting that requiring parents to pay for education might be a desirable method of imposing birth control on the poor, Friedman also proposed a "pay-for-use" model for education delivery:

> *Governments could require a minimum level of education which they could finance by giving parents vouchers redeemable for a specified maximum sum per child per year if spent on "approved" educational services. Parents would then be free to spend this sum and any additional sum on purchasing educational services from an "approved" institution of their own choice. The educational services could be rendered by private enterprises operated for profit, or by non-profit institutions of various kinds. The role of*

> *the government would be limited to assuring that the schools met certain minimum standards such as the inclusion of a minimum common content in their programs, much as it now inspects restaurants to assure that they maintain minimum sanitary standards.*[7]

This is the model of education that is avidly being promoted by groups like AIMS and the Fraser Institute, and which has widely been advanced in the United States. We will examine this model of educational delivery more closely in Chapter 5.

Although the idea of applying neoliberal tenets to education was formed in the earliest days of the neoliberal movement, it was not until Ronald Reagan took office that this dogma took root. In 1983, a report on America's schools was released from a group called the National Commission on Excellence in Education. Tellingly entitled *A Nation at Risk: The Imperative for Educational Reform*, this document set the tone of discourse that would dominate public education policy for years to come.[8]

The commission had been set up in 1981 at the request of then secretary of education Terrell Howard Bell to address what he saw as "the widespread public perception that something is seriously remiss [sic] in our education system," and to respond to that perception by examining the problems of American public education and proposing solutions.[9] The report was to address six topics:

- Assessing the quality of teaching and learning in [the] Nation's public and private schools, colleges, and universities;

- Comparing American schools and colleges with those of other advanced nations;

- Studying the relationship between college admissions requirements and student achievement in high school;

- Identifying educational programs which result in notable student success in college;

- Assessing the degree to which major social and educational changes in the last quarter century [had] affected student achievement; and

- Defining problems which must be faced and overcome if [Americans were] successfully to pursue the course of excellence in education.[10]

Probably the most interesting element of *A Nation at Risk* is that the document approached the education system from a deficit standpoint, endeavouring to "fix" an education system that had been predetermined as having been broken. This is what I call the Unsupported Deficiency Syndrome, and it would become a hallmark of the reformist movement for the next four decades.

The commission's eighteen-month study looked at a number of academic papers, held public consultations, reviewed analyses of problems in the system and drew information from a wide variety of other sources. To get a sense of the end result of this undertaking, one need only read the report's opening paragraph:

> *Our Nation is at risk. Our once unchallenged preeminence in commerce, industry, science, and technological innovation is being overtaken by competitors throughout the world. This report is concerned with only one of the many causes and dimensions of the problem, but it is the one that undergirds American prosperity, security, and civility. We report to the American people that while we can take justifiable pride in what our schools and colleges have historically accomplished and contributed to the United States and the well-being*

of its people, the educational foundations of our society are presently being eroded by a rising tide of mediocrity that threatens our very future as a Nation and a people. What was unimaginable a generation ago has begun to occur — others are matching and surpassing our educational attainments.[11]

The impact *A Nation at Risk* had on American schools cannot be overstated. Although the document has been widely criticized — with various academics citing everything from data error to a concern that the initial panel only contained one classroom teacher and no educational experts — the ideology it expressed quickly took hold. Educating American children was now no longer simply a matter of a social good and raising up the masses. According to *A Nation at Risk*, the reason for so many of the economic woes facing the country at the time was that public schools were failing the American people. With more than a hint of Fear, Uncertainty and Doubt (FUD), the commission made education a competitive race with nothing less than the fate of the nation at stake. And it was a race that America was losing.

By the 1990s, the next piece in the American educational reform puzzle emerged. In 1994, William Spady developed "outcome based education," which argued that all education could be broken down into outcomes — lists of things that students should be able to know and do by the end of a certain grade level or unit of study.[12] Through this approach, Spady envisioned education moving from "traditional" into "transformational," with students demonstrating their learning through high-stakes, performance-based assessments.

Jurisdictions began to adopt this movement and develop outcomes for various subjects, and, of course, expected teachers to teach to them. The problem was that different jurisdictions began the process with different outcomes. It soon became apparent that, in order to meet the desire to compare schools, outcomes across jurisdictions would need to become similar.

Thus, as the 1990s progressed into the new millennium, more of the policy developments by educational bureaucracies focused on standardization. However, if you are going to measure standard outcomes, you need a standard tool by which to do so. Before long, standardized tests became, well, the standard.

Nothing in education ever happens in a vacuum, and many of these changes and approaches were paralleled across the globe. As public appetite for determining educational performance increased, so too did the desire for methods of comparison. After all, it is one thing to think a particular jurisdiction is doing a great job of, for example, teaching math, but if you have no means of measuring performance or of comparing students, then you have no proof. What was needed, on an international scale, was a way to compare not just students within countries, but across them.

Enter the Organisation for Economic Co-operation and Development, better known as the OECD. Founded in 1961, the OECD was envisioned as a "new way forward" for European unity after the Second World War where countries would co-operate economically to more efficiently and effectively reconstruct a devastated continent.[13] Although meant to be an economic agency, the organization began to seriously turn its attention toward education in the 1990s.

In many countries, business groups had been making the connection between education and the workforce for years, as evidenced by *A Nation at Risk*. The OECD was also attuned to the connection. There was, for many, a direct correlation between how well a particular country was educating its youth and its potential for economic productivity: If you have a vibrant and productive school system, then you are presumably producing a vibrant and productive workforce. Building on this notion that educational excellence would lead to economic prosperity, the organization addressed the question of how that excellence could be measured. In 2000, the OECD launched the Programme for International Student Assessment (PISA) test onto an unsuspecting world.[14]

The idea behind these tests was simple. The OECD would develop a common assessment of student ability in three key subject areas: reading, science and math. They would distribute these tests internationally to member countries, where they would be written by fifteen-year-old students under similar conditions. The tests would be marked, and the resulting data would be collated and released.

For those who had been seeking a way to measure the performance of their education systems and to compare them, this was the perfect device. Before long, PISA became *the* measure of the ability of a nation to educate its children. Jurisdictions that scored highly were the toast of the international educational community, while those that did not saw their systems shaken to their very foundations.

One of the key elements of the initiative is that it uses very simple, easy-to-read graphs to report some very complex information. The resulting visuals often relay data in a somewhat skewed fashion, with jurisdictional scores that may be within a few percentage points of each other seeming to denote major differences. The overall scores of the various regions are often visually displayed as stacked, one on top of the other, allowing for a quick snapshot of each country's performance. Regardless of proximity on the scoring scale, the focus of the data is comparison. The top performers may only be a few percentage points ahead of the country in fifteenth place, but in a stack of, say, sixty segments of data, fifteenth is pretty far from the top. For example, in this graphic representation of the 2012 results, the difference between the highest placing OECD member country (indicated by bold text), Korea, and say, tenth place Germany is approximately 7 per cent.

Table 1: Mathematics performance among PISA 2012 participants, at national and regional levels

	Mean score	Range of ranks — All countries/economies Upper rank	Range of ranks — All countries/economies Lower rank
Shanghai-China	613	1	1
Singapore	573	2	2
Hong Kong-China	561	3	5
Chinese Taipei	560	3	5
Korea	554	3	5
Macao-China	538	6	8
Japan	536	6	9
Liechtenstein	535	6	9
Switzerland	531	7	9
Flemish community (Belgium)	531		
Trento (Italy)	524		
Friuli Venezia Giulia (Italy)	523		
Netherlands	523	9	14
Veneto (Italy)	523		
Estonia	521	10	14
Finland	519	10	15
Canada	518	11	16
Australian capital territory (Australia)	518		
Poland	518	10	17
Lombardy (Italy)	517		
Navarre (Spain)	517		
Western Australia (Australia)	516		
Belgium	515	13	17
Germany	514	13	17

Source: OECD/PISA (2014), *PISA 2012 Results in Focus: What 15-year-olds know and what they can do with what they know*, page 10.

Almost overnight, and despite this inherent shortcoming, PISA scores became the darling of the educational airwaves. The digestibility of a simple graph lent itself well to popular media, and, of course, popular commentary. What was often missing from that commentary, however, was a critical examination of the numbers. The PISA data are dissected more thoroughly by the OECD in the reports that accompany the results, including examinations of everything from how areas perform in teaching different genders to how they are doing teaching across socio-economic lines. This information often provides a very different picture of how well or how poorly a particular area is doing, but, rather unfortunately, seldom merits much more than a footnote in media reports. In the end, no matter how close the gender gap or how equitable the system, headlines inevitably focus on where jurisdictions place.

This focus on test scores, which had started to take root in the 1990s, was amplified when the first PISA scores were released in 2001 and American students placed right in the middle of the pack. Any perception that this was good enough, or that the US had not fully bought into the connection between education, competition and economics, was laid to rest in short order by then US secretary of education Rod Paige. In a press release about the results he stated, "In the global economy, these countries are our competitors — average is not good enough for American kids."[15]

Fortunately for these same American kids, the US Department of Education had a plan. In 2001, an act "to close the achievement gap with accountability, flexibility, and choice, so that no child is left behind" was introduced into the House of Representatives. It was signed into law in 2002 by President George W. Bush, and became known as the *No Child Left Behind Act* (*NCLB*).[16]

In essence, *NCLB* changed the purpose of standardized testing. Instead of being part of the school system, standardized test scores essentially became the very reason *for* the school system. Where once these tests had only been used to measure student performance, they became part of a wide-sweeping focus on school and, more specifically, teacher capability. The basic intent of public education was redefined to build on the idea of standardized outcomes and to improve achievement of those outcomes by focusing upon them to a greater extent.

In order to achieve this focus, the *NCLB* movement took a fairly radical step. The authors of the document concluded that tests scores should be tied to school funding. If a state wished to access federal money for education, they would need to develop and use these standardized tests. Furthermore, the individual schools within that state were expected not only to use these tests, but to improve their results each year.

The *Act* went further to state that if schools did not improve in consecutive years, they could officially be deemed as "in need of improvement." If standardized test scores still did not improve, the school would be subject to even closer scrutiny and could suffer any number of consequences, including reduced funding, replacing of some (or all) of the staff or even closure.

The test scores were used as a way of identifying both underperforming schools and teachers. If an individual teacher's test scores were not up to expectations, they could be disciplined and even fired. The same was true of administrators who were deemed ultimately responsible for student achievement. Suffice it to say this created a tremendous amount of motivation for (and pressure placed upon) teachers to improve these scores. At the same time, the US began to expand the use of school-choice policies, where parents were able to send their children to schools of their own choosing using a voucher system. Each parent was granted a voucher equal to the amount of money that would have been given to the local public school, and was allowed to spend that money on any state-approved educational option. Often, one of the key determinants in deciding which schools were "better" were these test results. This idea of schools competing for students and, by extension, teachers having to compete for their jobs, and the use of a school voucher system followed almost exactly the educational vision of Milton Friedman from fifty years before.

With the election of Barack Obama in 2008, there was hope that this obsession with standardized scores would fade, but that hope was dashed when Obama announced his own take on educational reform, dubbed "Race to the Top."[17] Again closely tied to economics, this reform expanded the criteria through which schools and teachers could demonstrate excellence and again saw education dollars tied to these criteria. It also saw increased emphasis on the notion of tying teacher performance to student test scores. If students' test scores did not increase, teachers could be fired. In schools where scores did increase, teachers could be offered cash bonuses. The incentive to increase test scores by any means necessary led to some rather questionable practices in many US jurisdictions, including everything from accusations of test doctoring to outright cheating scandals.

* * *

In Canada we were not immune to the impacts of these movements. Much like in America, the early 1990s was a time of great focus on the economics of education. The dialogue around schools and how they were failing to prepare the next generation of students for the workforce reached such a pitch that it inspired a rebuttal book, entitled *Class Warfare: The Assault on Canada's Schools*.[18] Written in 1994 by Maude Barlow, chairperson of the Council of Canadians, and Heather-Jane Robertson, an executive member of the Canadian Centre for Policy Alternatives, the book became a bestseller. According to the authors, the outcry over Canada's supposedly "mediocre" education system was not based on facts, but was a myth perpetuated by those who saw education as a market opportunity and who were using FUD — Fear, Uncertainty and Doubt — to call the capabilities of the current system into question.

If you want a sense of just how repetitive education history can be, *Class Warfare* is the place to start. The authors discuss some of the edu-myths of the time and spend considerable effort debunking them. That the myths themselves sound so familiar in today's context gives a sense of their pervasiveness and the tenacity with which the neoliberal think tanks have stuck to their messaging. Chapter titles such as "Myth 1: Our Schools Have Failed Us ... and Our Kids" and "Myth 2: Our Graduates Just Don't Have the Skills" show that little has changed in twenty-five years of educational discourse. For example, the authors at one point discuss a claim by businesses that they needed to be aware of Canada's poor showing on international assessments. However, the test that was being referred to, the Second International Assessment of Educational Progress, actually showed that Canada was either as good as or better than every other country that had taken the test. Despite this strong showing, one of Canada's top national publications, *MacLean's* magazine, ran a special report in January 1993 entitled "What's Wrong at School?"[19] Unsupported Deficiency Syndrome, it seems, is not a new phenomenon.

In Nova Scotia, we were not spared this swell of reformation driven by a desire to measure and compare. In 1994, the Atlantic Provinces set up the Atlantic Provinces Education Foundation (APEF), which was established to determine a common-core curriculum across all the Atlantic Provinces in English, math, science, social studies and technology.[20] This standardization thrust sought to establish common outcomes across all the subjects, with each document being developed under the umbrella of what were known as Essential Graduation Learnings (EGLs).

These EGLs were very large ideas and spoke to the overall purpose of public education. They included such overarching ideas as "aesthetic expression," "citizenship" and "personal development." The foundation documents and the accompanying curriculum guides were created with the input of educators from around the region and provided many classroom-based ideas for teachers. The framework they provided was, in many ways, focused on developing the whole student.

In the words of the foundation documents themselves, they had been designed to:

- Improve the quality of education for all students through shared expertise and resources

- Ensure that the education students receive across the region is equitable

- Meet the needs of both students and society[21]

What was noticeably absent from these documents was the deficiency language that had crept into so many other comparable documents. There was no suggestion that schools were failing or that the scores on tests would be tied to school funding or teacher evaluations. Indeed, if there is a "right way" to standardize curricula, this model from Atlantic Canada circa 1994 is the closest to how that process should unfold.

Although this standardization movement did not have the teeth that it had in the US, there were still concerns raised in the mid-1990s by teacher organizations, including the Nova Scotia Teachers Union, about what was happening.[22] It is interesting how many of these early fears, some of which seemed rather alarmist at the time, eventually came to be realized. The major concern was that the test results would be used to compare teachers, and the union was insistent that these tests not become part of the teachers' performance evaluations. There were also questions about why change was even necessary, and about the extent to which what was essential upon graduation could be standardized and still remain culturally responsive to minority communities. There was also some concern raised about the danger to marginalized students, since even in these early stages researchers were aware they could be particularly disadvantaged by standardized tests. In spite of these reservations, standardization and, more specifically, the teaching of outcomes soon became the norm in Nova Scotia. The first provincially standardized exam inspired by the new outcomes-based curriculum was given to students in Nova Scotia at the same time that the OECD was first distributing the PISA test.

* * *

We've traced the origin of some of the major reform ideas that are impacting education systems, but this is not an exhaustive treatment. My intent is to offer a basic introduction to some of the historically relevant and influential events that are still having an impact today. Even as these events were unfolding, few noticed any connection between the changes in the education system and the ideology of neoliberalism. Education is, by its very nature, a fluid endeavour, and much of the change that was taking place seemed, if not completely benign, at least relatively harmless. As standards and standardization became more normalized, there was very little serious resistance to their implementation.

There was, however, a certain sense of unease creeping into the teaching profession. As the rhetoric around accountability and comparison increased, teachers began to feel targeted. As the think tanks continued to promote their story of failing educational systems via the Unsupported Deficiency Syndrome, they simultaneously vilified teachers, and more specifically their unions, as impediments to meaningful educational change. As news outlets reported on falling tests scores and "poor" test results, teachers often heard nothing but bad news about their work.

As the neoliberal ideology spread across the globe with public education as a focus, many jurisdictions saw tremendous increases in calls for change. Since schools were failing, well-meaning individuals began to call for reform. These calls were often very loud and very public and echoed the neoliberal ideals of increasing competition between schools and opening the education system up to free-market forces.

These reformers influenced the global discourse about education through a movement that became somewhat disparagingly known as GERM.

CHAPTER 3
The Global Education Reform Movement (2000–2010)

The Canadian school system has proven resistant to many of the ill-fated educational trends that have emerged south of the border. However, almost everything America does has a global impact, and educational ideology is no exception. Across the globe, education systems are experiencing surprisingly similar trends with unfortunately dubious results.

The neoliberal prescription for public education reform was, for the longest time, missing an identifying moniker. Educators were being subjected to various versions of this ideology but couldn't quite put their finger on what was happening, or, more importantly, why. As standardization became more pervasive and schools were held more accountable for measuring student achievement, everyone within the system recognized that things were changing. But where, many teachers asked themselves, was the impetus for change coming from?

The answer to that question came, somewhat unexpectedly, from Finland. In 2011, the director of the Finnish Ministry of Education and Culture, Pasi Sahlberg, released a book entitled *Finnish Lessons: What Can the World Learn from Educational*

Change in Finland?[1] This book is a must-read for anyone interested in understanding modern educational reform. In the early 2000s, Finland, a country of less than six million people, emerged as an educational powerhouse, scoring consistently well on international assessments such as PISA. This led to questioning what, precisely, Finland was doing to achieve these impressive results. Sahlberg's book identified a number of key contributing factors, including a major reformation of the Finnish education system that began in the 1970s. At that time, Finland adopted what was then a revolutionary idea that, given the appropriate support and opportunities, all students can learn, as opposed to the more traditional view that certain students were unable to learn certain things. They took much of the emphasis away from the competitive nature of education that had previously existed in the country and made the system more collective. Instead of adopting strategies and policies from other jurisdictions, Finland developed a distinctly "Finnish way" of educating its population.

This was a fundamental theme of Sahlberg's work: that nations should develop their own systems of success rather than adopting a one-size-fits-all ideology promoted globally by educational reformists. It was also Sahlberg who described what was happening and coined a term for it. His term, Global Education Reform Movement, more commonly referred to as GERM, entered the lexicon.

According to Sahlberg, GERM "evolves from the increased international exchange of policies and practices. It is not a formal global policy program, but rather an unofficial education agenda that relies on a certain set of assumptions to improve education systems."[2] He argued that as the globalization of education increased, there was an accompanying increase in pressure upon schools to adopt a more results-based, measurable model of education. This, according to the author, was being driven by a business-based (read: neoliberal) ideology, which held that school success could be measured by the quality of the products produced — in this case the students.

Sahlberg pointed out that GERM had been driven by three separate but interrelated factors that had been at play since the 1980s, the decade that had seen the rise of Thatcherism and Reaganism. The first was a shift in the paradigm of education from a focus on teaching to a focus on learning. What students learned, or rather how well they learned it, became the dominant driver in schools, as opposed to what was to be taught. This was accompanied by an increased focus on numeracy and literacy skills, and the measurement thereof, much to the detriment of other skill sets. The second factor was a sudden uptick in demand from the public for a quality education for all students. A sense developed that all students were entitled to a quality education, and models of inclusion became the norm, as did the institution of learning standards. Third, Sahlberg identified an increase in the adoption of competition and accountability measures for schools, and the accompanying assumption of this being a positive step, as the final component to the movement. There is a strong belief among those who support GERM ideology that having schools compete against each other for funding, and even for students, results in better overall outcomes for everyone. As Sahlberg described it, GERM was very much an expression of the neoliberal ideologies grounded in the theories of Hayek and Friedman.

Using these three factors as a basis, Sahlberg identified five common features of the GERM movement that provided a framework to test for the pervasiveness of the condition. Essentially, if an education system has all five "symptoms," it can be said to have come down with GERM.

The first symptom is an increased focus on standardization, and use of standardized tests. With the wide acceptance of outcome-based education, there is a correlated acceptance that the focus in the classroom should shift from what is taught to how well things are learned. Outcomes can be standardized across jurisdictions, ensuring that every child, regardless of where they go to school, learns the same things. GERM ideology posits that if jurisdictions set sufficiently high standards, and make those learning outcomes clear for everyone, then achievement *will* improve. However, the only way to ensure that this improvement has been realized is to test the results. These tests are a core component of GERM, with results being used for everything from determining funding for schools to salary bonuses for teachers.

This first symptom leads almost naturally to the second. Jurisdictions that are experiencing the impact of GERM increase their focus on core subjects, specifically those involving literacy and numeracy — to the detriment of the arts and social sciences. In Sahlberg's own words, "Due to the acceptance of international student assessments . . . as criteria for educational performance, reading, mathematical and scientific literacy have now become the main determinants of perceived success or failure of pupils, teachers, schools and entire education systems."[3]

The third symptom of GERM centres around curriculum and, more specifically, a narrowing of educational focus. Essentially, if the test becomes the measure of excellence for a system, then teaching to the test is a logical result. The downside is that both teaching and learning necessarily become more constrained, particularly when the tests are considered "high stakes." After all, if a teacher's job is connected to their students' test scores, then it is doubtful that they will spend a great deal of class time focusing on anything else. This leads to a less enriching learning environment and seizing the teachable moment becomes a thing of the past.

The fourth characteristic of the GERM ideology addresses the connection between business interests and the classroom. When GERM is in play, educational policies and practices follow business models as opposed to educational ones. These policies are often supported and, in some cases, promoted by private industry, professional consultants and wealthy philanthropists, but are recognizably devoid of the input of educators.

Sahlberg sees two major drawbacks with going outside of the system to develop educational policy. First, it limits a system's ability to improve its own processes and "an education system's own capability to maintain renewal," and second, it prevents the sort of cross-professional learning that is so key in developing and maintaining a successful education program.[4] It is hard, for example, for teachers to share some of the best practices they have developed around teaching a certain subject if how that subject is to be taught has been prescribed by an outside agency or if the education system is not set up to promote such exchange.

The final symptom of GERM is a culmination of all the others. It is a focus on accountability practices, specifically around student achievement, and includes such measures as accreditation policies for schools that are closely tied to improving student results. Schools that see improvement in tests scores are deemed to be successful and are rewarded; those where scores do not improve are punished. A parallel development that can occur here is the creation of accountability standards for teachers, where policy makers create "new and improved" accountability measures and evaluation tools to measure teacher effectiveness.

Of course, the general public and many parents will look at these tenets of GERM and wonder where the problem lies. If you break it down to a simple few sentences, you have a reform movement that wishes to focus on the core competencies of literacy and numeracy, test those competencies in students and hold both individuals and systems accountable when those competencies are not realized. On the surface, it seems to make a great deal of sense.

The problem is that it doesn't work.

To begin with, defining a set of standards — what should be taught and how teachers should teach — does not actually result in better achievement. The theory that setting standards and increasing accountability will automatically result in better outcomes for students simply does not hold up. GERM assumes that competition is inherently good for systems, as per the neoliberal worldview. If schools are forced to compete for students or for funding, that competition will naturally force schools to improve. This assumption is inaccurate, particularly in a public education system. Sharing resources and new teaching strategies is key to teacher professional development and for advancing student learning. Classroom teachers, schools, even whole jurisdictions naturally seek to exchange ideas around helping kids achieve. Any teacher who walks into a staffroom with questions on how to help a particular student or how to craft a better lesson will undoubtedly get as many suggestions as there are teachers in the room. However, in a competitive system, this free exchange of best practice is counterproductive. If having the best test scores in the district means continued funding, or if having the best test scores in the school means staying employed, there is little interest in sharing "trade secrets" that help students. One of Sahlberg's key explanations of why the Finnish system had seen so much success was that it had managed to avoid most of the GERM trends, especially around this notion of competition.

In 2009, Canadian academic Andy Hargreaves and Boston College education professor Dennis Shirley published *The Fourth Way: The Inspiring Future for Educational Change*, which provides a dissection of the GERM movement and some of its potential downfalls.[5] Referring to this marketized structure as "the Second Way," the authors point out that, "Despite undeniable benefits of clearer focus, greater consistency, and attention to all students ... the downsides of Second Way reforms were enormous."[6] These included a reduction in the depth and breadth of education, a decrease in teacher retention, an increase in drop-out rates and a stratification of the system, whereby the more affluent or educated parents, who understood how to navigate bureaucracies, saw the greatest benefits, to the detriment of those who did not.

Neoliberalism and GERM can have even more profound impacts on defining the very purpose of public education. When this ideology takes hold, people see themselves as products they are responsible for marketing. In order to enhance their individual marketability and to compete for jobs, individuals view the education system as knowing only one objective: it's seen as a means to get ahead financially. Students see school subjects only through the lens of future employment opportunities and earning potential. The discourse changes from school being about developing "the whole child" to seeing courses as "investments in the future."

This view of the overall purpose of education leads to the stratification of school courses. Students, parents and even teachers get caught up in the notion that some school subjects lend themselves more adequately to future financial success than others. Subjects such as math and science take on greater prestige than the humanities or the arts. This increased focus on employability has a twofold impact on schools. First, it leads to a narrowing of curricula, where schools rush to offer more credits in certain courses, to the detriment of supposedly "softer" classes. Second, those courses that do remain within a school's schedule may see a reduction in enrolment. In high school, for example, students find themselves under pressure to load up on science courses or pick up an advanced math credit, leaving little room within their day for courses such as drama, art or music.

Valuing certain ways of knowing can lead to narrowing choices even within the math, science and technology offerings. In Nova Scotia for example, students must successfully complete eighteen credits over the course of their three years in secondary school to graduate. Of these, thirteen are considered mandatory. Of these mandatory credits, three must be from the language arts strand, and six must be from math, science or technology. However, recent changes to the rules have seen full-year math credits introduced in Grade 10, and the 2019 school year saw the introduction of a mandatory Grade 12 math credit. The result is that students have less time for other more open-ended technology courses that would meet the graduation requirements. These include such courses as Skilled Trades, Film and Video Production or Computer Programming, to name a few.

Perhaps not surprisingly, this increased emphasis on certain courses lends itself well to the measurement of success rates. Major national and international assessment tools like PISA are almost exclusively designed around math, science and reading. A successful school system within the neoliberal framework is one that produces good student results in these three subjects. Other subjects are viewed as peripheral, and arts programs or physical education activities are valued principally for their ability to support the more measurable subjects. This is evidenced by the new trend in STEM (science, technology, engineering and math) education, now often changed to STEAM to allow for the inclusion of the arts within a supposedly more rigorous academic framework. The arts are permitted to share the timetable only inasmuch as they help students better understand and learn the other core subjects.

This peripheral damage may be difficult to see from outside of the system, but it is a logical result of the trend. If a school has been tasked with increasing focus on a competitive model, then focus must be taken away from more collective ends. This was recently demonstrated in Nova Scotia when it was suddenly announced in 2018 that library support staff were to be removed from elementary school libraries in the Cape Breton Region. Minister of Education Zach Churchill defended the move by saying that it was not about saving money, but about meeting the changing needs of students. He stated "the fact [is] that students are using traditional libraries less and less as technology changes . . . this is about ensuring that the education delivery model is always changing to meet the needs of our students."[7]

This rather dismissive assessment of the importance of school libraries is out of synch with the research. One study by the Ontario Library Association found that having a school librarian was "the single strongest predictor of reading enjoyment for both grade 3 and 6 students."[8] More recent studies have found that having a school librarian not only increased standardized test scores, but did so most impactfully for at-risk learners, including students from minority backgrounds.[9] Ensuring school libraries remained open and were perhaps expanded would be a more appropriate method of "meeting the needs of students."

This is an excellent example of how GERM, which attempts to sell itself as being about improving education, reveals its more authentic colours. Although I seriously doubt the intent of this decision was to harm children, GERM, by its very nature, causes a great deal of peripheral damage. Adding an extra math credit may look good in the papers, but there is little evidence to suggest that it will improve high-school graduation rates among the poor, or among any demographic for that matter. Cutting library programs and library staff that improve reading levels among the disenfranchised further separates the "haves" from the "have-nots" and reduces student achievements.

This consequence illustrates one of the main premises upon which the movement is founded. If you have winners, there will be losers. This tenet of neoliberalism holds in the economy too. A 2016 report from the International Monetary Fund on neoliberalism identified a number of what it called "disquieting conclusions"[10] about the ideology. The report found that the connection between the agenda and increased income inequality was quite clear. Indeed, rather than resulting in positive outcomes, the adoption of the neoliberal agenda hurt both "the level and the sustainability of growth."[11] No one would argue this is an outcome we want for our public schools.

One of the most publicized examples of the limited capacity for GERM-based initiatives to produce positive educational outcomes for students emerged in 2018. That year the think tank RAND (Research ANd Development) released a report on the efforts of the Bill and Melinda Gates Foundation to improve educational outcomes for both students and teachers in the US.[12] That initiative, called the Intensive Partnerships for Effective Teaching, saw the foundation recruit three school districts and four charter-school organizations who "agreed to develop a robust measure of teaching effectiveness, including a structured way to observe and assess classroom teaching."[13] These measures of teacher effectiveness relied on only two factors: classroom observations by administration and standardized testing of students. It also saw a merit-based pay system instituted where teachers who were deemed to have improved were paid more than those who had not. After several years and close to $1 billion in funding, the report concluded that the effort had failed to increase graduation rates or student achievement. Furthermore, the merit-based pay system did not result in retaining teachers, another goal of the project.

Other research has found that GERM-based policies and experimentation come up short in their promoted goal of improving outcomes for kids. And although the research of institutions like RAND and academics like Hargreaves have been able to point to lack of positive gains resulting from the trend, there has been little serious effort to consider the damage they have caused. The Gates Foundation efforts to identify effective teachers was presumably accompanied by an equal effort to label some of them ineffective. There is no data on careers that were ended when individual educators failed to "meet the mark" set by a system that would eventually be proven to be of little use to students.

More concerning is the impact that these GERM experiments have on students themselves. The teachers who were deemed "effective" by the Gates Foundation failed to improve results for students on standardized tests, but we have no way of knowing what that hyper-focus on testing cost those students in other areas. The RAND report says that there were no measurable gains in test scores, but I wonder what was lost because the teachers were under pressure to teach to the test. I can think of no other area in society where experimentation would be carried out on our children without some understanding, or at the very least, consideration, of the negative side effects.

This is why GERM is so concerning for those of us who want public education to remain in the public realm. We all recognize it as an imperfect system, but it is a system with a track record of relative success for most students. Beyond the potential of GERM to lead to a system which prioritizes profit over pupils, there is alarm to be raised around the potential damage that will be done. This damage is not just limited to the schools directly impacted by the efforts of wealthy philanthropists. The ideas of measuring schools based on their standardized tests score and "new and improved" teacher accountability practices are alive and well within the public system. The more these efforts are promoted and pursued, the more energy and effort they require. If unchecked, this trend will result in teachers spending even more time meeting some artificial measure of competency and even less time working with their students.

This is a cursory look at two complex and intertwined ideologies that are driving current educational change across the globe. A number of authors, including Sahlberg, have dedicated entire volumes to the rise of GERM, and the theory and practice of neoliberalism could take up a considerable portion of any bookshelf. But when discussing the current education system in Nova Scotia, it is important to understand the global context.

The ideas of neoliberalism probably sound familiar and, indeed, they have become so pervasive that, in some cases, they have been accepted as the way things should be. You need look no further than your local public school for evidence of this. Increased standardized testing, calls for more stringent teacher evaluations and the implementation of full-year math programs are just some of the trends that point to the creep of GERM into our system. The manner in which these developments are not just accepted but actively promoted and pursued give a sense of the extent of our current adoption of GERM thinking. The next chapter will look at some of the major educational policy thrusts of the past twenty-five years, with an eye to establishing how our system has been changing to adapt, and how Nova Scotia came down with such a bad case of GERM.

CHAPTER 4
Connecting Education and Employability (1990–2010)

Over the course my career, I have met a wide variety of people involved in education, one of whom was Dr. Pamela Rogers. I met Rogers when she was working on her doctorate at the University of Ottawa on the topic of neoliberalism and its impact on the Nova Scotia education system. This chapter relies heavily on her research and her thesis "Tracing Neoliberal Governmentality in Education: Disentangling Economic Crises, Accountability, and the Disappearance of Social Studies."[1]

To understand how our education system has been impacted by neoliberalism, we need to go back to the early 1990s. The Nova Scotia economy was in the spotlight, deficits were on the rise, the population was aging and declining and many young people were "going down the road" to gain employment elsewhere. It was during these years that the discourse around education changed to include ideas of accountability, testing and competition that flow from neoliberalism and GERM.

The Comparison Imperative: Global Competitiveness and Employability

The 1990s were a particularly turbulent time for education in Nova Scotia. Under Premier John Savage, the Liberal government had won a strong majority in the 1993 election, taking forty-one of the province's fifty-two seats. Many governmental policies of the 1990s revolved around reducing deficits and opening up markets to spur growth, and Savage followed this trend. Almost immediately after taking power, he introduced a series of austerity measures including what would forever be known as "Savage days," where public-sector employees were forced to take unpaid holidays in order to cut government wage costs.[2]

During this time two reports were published that set the tone for educational discourse. The first was the 1994 policy document *Restructuring Nova Scotia's Education System, Preparing Students for a Lifetime of Learning*,[3] and the second was the 1995 *Education Horizons: White Paper on Restructuring the Education System*.[4] Both called on the Nova Scotia education system to change in response to global economic forces. The documents spoke of a need to accelerate the shift away from a resource-based economy to a more knowledge-based one, and warned that without such a shift, Nova Scotia was in danger of "falling behind." Our education system, it was reasoned, needed to prepare students for the impending and inevitable drastic changes in the job market.

Rogers notes the tone of these documents. In any call for improvement, there is an inherent implication that what we are currently doing is not "good enough." According to Rogers, "The tone . . . is important to note, as it strategically positions Nova Scotia on the periphery to 'the global' . . . there was a reactionary impetus for the province to not fall behind the rest of the world."[5]

There was relatively little empirical evidence to suggest that Nova Scotia students were not already being prepared for the impending shift. However, even in these early stages of the reform movement, Unsupported Deficiency Syndrome was already being perpetuated. Both reports quoted national and international assessment scores to bolster the call to action. The messaging was clear: Nova Scotia's education system was a means by which the province could lift itself out of its economic malaise. Unless students were equipped with the appropriate competencies, we were abandoning hope of our young people being able to compete in a global job market.

An interesting element of these two documents is their evolving visions of the purpose of public education. *Restructuring* talks about the value of making students lifelong learners and the importance of personal growth, but at the same time references the importance of employability skills such as teamwork and problem solving. With the release of *Horizons*, policy makers increased their emphasis on bringing about economic stability and growth through ensuring that students developed their workplace skills as opposed to focusing on personal growth.[6]

It is noteworthy that *Horizons* declared unequivocally that Nova Scotia's "graduates lack the basic skills required in the global marketplace." That is exactly the type of alarmist rhetoric that *Class Warfare* had attempted to refute in 1994 and that echoes *A Nation at Risk* from a decade before. That this sentiment remains part of the conversation around education even in 2020, void of any substantive supportive evidence, speaks to the power of repetitive messaging. Rogers sums up the overall sense of urgency and the alleged failure of our system by highlighting the following summary statement from *Horizons*:

> *If Nova Scotia is to compete successfully in the global economy, our education system must be strong enough to support the needs of our communities and flexible enough to change with them. We cannot serve the needs of future generations by standing still.*[7]

After two successive Liberal governments, Nova Scotia ushered in the Progressive Conservatives in 1999 under Dr. John Hamm (1999–

2006) and then Rodney MacDonald (2006–09). During this time, the government introduced a number of policy documents dealing with education, and the tone of the discourse softened. Although there was more optimism, there was still a strong connection made between economic prosperity and education. In fact, during his election campaign, Hamm often stated that our schools primarily needed to prepare young people for future job markets.[8]

Although they were perhaps not quite as vocal about the economic concerns around education, the Hamm years did provide some tense moments when it came to public-sector spending. Within the first few months, the government appointed a fiscal management team to embark on a complete program review. The team held public consultations across the province and released its interim report at the end of 1999, which called for the elimination of the province's deficit within two years and asked departments to prepare budgets that would reflect cuts of up to 30 per cent.[9]

As a result of this exercise, it was projected that over 700 teaching positions would be lost and approximately 1,100 support staff would, potentially, be let go. This led to a series of protests and, within days, teachers, parents and students showed their concern through letter-writing, email campaigns and rallies. Eventually the government made some concessions and massive cuts were avoided, but even in this relatively optimistic period in Nova Scotia's history, neoliberal ideas were appearing in the political discourse — in particular the inherent value of reducing public-sector spending.

The majority of government educational documents produced under the Conservatives retained the tone of optimism and conveyed a sense that education could be a vehicle for achieving a brighter future for Nova Scotia. Markedly downplayed were any claims that schools were not already preparing students to achieve their best. There was little discussion around the global economy or a sense that our young people would not be able to compete. However, this changed in 2005.

That year the provincial Tories produced a policy document entitled *Learning for Life II: Brighter Futures Together*, which called for an infusion of about $22 million into the education system.[10] The government was responding to what it referred to as "input from education partners" and stated that it wished to enact changes to ensure that "all students graduate with the best possible preparation for their futures." Again, there was a focus on the future and a better tomorrow, but the document differed from previous Tory reports in that it spoke not only of preparing students to do well at home, but also to participate in the "global economy."

This was a particularly interesting development in that it echoed the neoliberal idea that education was inherently connected to economics. Much had been made of this connection by the NDP government in Ontario in the late 1990s under Premier Bob Rae, when that government emphasized "the need to link education more closely to the world of work through stronger partnerships between government, business and labour."[11] This was further emphasized by the Conservative government of Mike Harris during his turbulent years in power. That this ideology had crossed party lines in multiple provinces was an early sign of the extent to which it had permeated the general psyche. It did not seem to matter who was in power, education and competing globally were inextricably linked.

Brighter Futures divided the overall goal of improving student achievement into two broad categories: raising the bar and closing the gap. The division here was key in that raising the bar dealt with students who might be more academically inclined and saw funding channelled to such programs as the International Baccalaureate (IB) program and increased access to French immersion. Closing the gap dealt with programming for students who might not be as academically inclined and saw an increased focus on skills and trades training. These included the development of the Options and Opportunities program, which was specifically targeted toward students who wished to pursue a career in the trades.[12]

This was a pivotal moment for education in Nova Scotia. This was the first policy document to develop a plan for students to follow different "routes" through school, depending upon student interest and level of academic success.[13] During the 1970s and '80s, it had been standard practice for students to be streamed according to the level of academic achievement their teachers expected them to attain. Many of these practices were subsequently determined to be damaging to students and were abandoned in the early 1990s. With the development of specialized in-school programming, the education system was again able to offer a variety of optional streams to students, while avoiding much of the criticism associated with streaming as an official practice. As programs became more established, individual student choice and parent advocacy, as opposed to academic standing, came to play a greater role in determining educational pathways.

The expansion of the IB Diploma Program, which had been almost exclusively within the purview of private schools, was meant to appeal to students who were planning on pursuing a post-secondary education. Described as a "rigorous pre-university course of studies," IB was originally established in Europe in 1968 as a way of creating a common course of study and university entry credentialing for students moving from one country to another. Courses in the two-year program require a higher level of academic commitment than regular school programming and class sizes are typically small. Students are assessed on the completion of demanding coursework and on a standardized, externally developed exam. With *Brighter Futures*, Nova Scotia went from having two schools that offered IB courses to twelve. The Department of Education boasted that "no other province or state has launched the IB Diploma Program in so many schools at one time."[14] This provided an element of choice for parents and allowed academically ambitious students access to a more challenging and potentially rewarding high-school education.

Other schools achieved a similar result by increasing emphasis on academically advanced courses through the Advanced Placement (AP) Program. Advanced Placement students take university-level courses and achieve credits toward their post-secondary degree while they are still in high school. Course guidelines are set out by an organization known as the College Board, an international not-for-profit that exists to make connections between universities and high-school students. Advanced Placement credits are recognized by most, if not all, universities across Canada and the United States. Schools can offer either IB or AP courses, but not both.

Further opportunity for program selection was achieved with the expansion of French immersion programming, which, like AP, predated *Brighter Futures* by a considerable margin. The idea of offering English-speaking students a separate French-speaking stream through the public education system originated in the 1960s during Quebec's "Quiet Revolution." At root was the rising importance of the French language in Quebec, and the idea that students would need to speak French fluently in order to achieve "social and economic success in the province."[15] Although the offering of French language instruction had been sold as a way to national unity and was enshrined in the *Official Languages Act* of 1969, even in 2016–17 the percentage of students enrolled in these programs varied significantly across the country, from 7 per cent in Alberta to 29 per cent in New Brunswick. In Nova Scotia, the figure was 17 per cent, above the national average of 11 per cent.[16]

The benefits of learning a second language are well documented, with research showing positive gains in everything from academic skills like problem solving and communication to students developing a more enhanced sense of empathy toward others and a greater sense of social justice.[17] Research into the benefits of French immersion, however, has not been quite as conclusive. Although it has been shown that immersion results in greater functional proficiency in French compared to conventional second-language instruction methods, there is some question around the capacity of the program to help students "attain native-like grammatical accuracy."[18] There has also been criticism that the program is another way for resourceful parents to effectively stream their children within the public-school system. A 2015 report in *Maclean's* magazine concluded that French immersion "has become an elitist, overly restrictive system, geared to benefit a certain type of student."[19] With the expansion of French immersion programs in Nova Scotia, *Brighter Futures* again reinforced the notion that regular public schooling could not ensure the best educational outcomes and laid out an alternative path for upwardly mobile students.

For students who were not academically inclined, the Options and Opportunities (O_2) program was offered as yet another "stream," this one envisioned for those who were going into the workforce or entering trades training after high school. This program also offers courses beyond traditional high-school classes, but rather than taking academic courses and writing external exams, students are given on-the-job training through an extensive co-operative program. Program participants go out into the workforce and gain high-school completion credits based on the success of that work experience. Thus, according to Rogers: "With the distinctions between academically motivated students for the province to 'raise the bar,' in the IB program, and all other students lumped together in 'closing the gap,' *Brighter Futures* (2005) coupled certain economic futures (globally minded, professionals versus trades workers) to education programming."[20]

While this shift in programming was being developed for students, *Brighter Futures* simultaneously presented a fundamentally different vision of the role of teachers. With an increased emphasis on numeracy and literacy, *Brighter Futures* marked a move away from such holistic goals as building relationships with students to a more data driven model.[21] This included implementation of the teacher professional growth plan, a document produced by teachers in which they were required to outline how they were going to improve their professional practice each year. These plans were to be read and approved by administration and were kept on file. If plans were deemed lacking by the administration, teachers were required to change them. It was also at this time that the department suggested that a province-wide school monitoring system should be created, which would replace teacher-developed marking systems. Although this goal was not achieved until the introduction of PowerSchool in 2010,[22] both these developments marked a significant reduction in the professional autonomy of teachers and an increased emphasis on their accountability.

Brighter Futures solidified the connection between school and employment within Nova Scotian public-education policy. Although many of the programming reforms were widely applauded by parents and teachers alike, they represented a subtle but solid change in the perception of the purpose of public education. The programs may have been introduced with different intentions, but the result was that parents began to view schools through a "marketplace" lens. Schools that offered IB programs, for example, could boast about being internationally accredited while others could not. Schools that offered French immersion became more valued than those that did not. Given options, parents could enroll their children in schools based on the programs they offered, not because of any sort of intrinsic value, but for their potential to improve their children's future employability. This led to the development of a critical view of "regular" school programming. Students who were not taking IB courses or who were not enrolled in French immersion programming were viewed as having an education that was somehow "less than" those who were.

In many ways, *Brighter Futures* can be viewed as a politically perfect educational document. It allowed the government of the day to position itself as offering solutions to what it had portrayed as a foundering education system by emphasizing choice within the system. At the same time, it instituted a series of accountability measures for teachers, which it could point to as a means of improving schools. By promoting the use of data and standardized assessment, it was able to boast that school success (or lack thereof) could now be measured and reported on in the public eye. This report and the ideology that it represented became the primary driver of educational discourse in Nova Scotia for well over a decade, and still resonates strongly.

Although there had been less focus on competing in the global marketplace between 1999 and 2005, there was widespread attention paid to educational standardization. The Atlantic Provinces Education Federation (APEF) began to explore the idea of creating a common-core curriculum across all four Atlantic Provinces. The objective was the development of a common curriculum based on an agreed upon set of Essential Graduation Learnings (EGLs), as discussed in Chapter 2. These curricula would have common assessments so that jurisdictions could compare how well they were meeting the outcomes. In Nova Scotia, this resulted in the creation of common Grade 12 exams, which were distributed across the province once per semester. The results of these tests were disseminated on a board-by-board basis, to enable jurisdictions to compare their results. Although the discourse in this period did not stress global competition, there was still a pervading wish to know how our students were doing in comparison to others and a tremendous focus on schools as a means through which students should gain employability skills.

The NDP government, elected to a majority in 2009 under Darrell Dexter, did not institute any major educational reforms, however, Rogers notes that they continued to advance the ideas that had preceded them. They expanded the notion of trades training, and they echoed the sentiment of previous governments when it came to the purpose of public education. Emboldened by the awarding of a major federal shipbuilding contract to the province, the government rhetoric continued the message of how education was the best way for students to achieve the skills necessary to compete in the global marketplace. That all three major political parties had adopted a similar educational policy spoke strongly of the pervasiveness of that view of public education's main purpose.

As our schools moved into the twenty-first century, the connection between education and employability was well entrenched in Nova Scotia. With the introduction of the provincial exam (as well as several other provincial grade-level assessments) the system was quietly being changed from the top down to reflect the ideas of the neoliberal movement. And much as these twenty-five years or so had set Nova Scotia up to believe education was all about competing for jobs, there was another development underway that solidified adoption of the global educational reform agenda.

The Improvement Imperative: Data Collection and the Push for Accountability

In 2002, the Halifax Regional School Board (HRSB), the province's largest, appointed Carole Olsen to the position of superintendent. Olsen, who had previously worked for the Toronto District School Board and the Ontario Ministry of Education, lost no time in sharing her vision of public education. During her first few months in the position, Olsen went from building to building asking principals two key questions: "How is your school doing?" and "How do you know?" It soon became clear that in the absence of data there was no way school leaders could authentically report that they were doing a good job of educating their students.

This approach reflected the shift in educational philosophy being experienced in the region at the time. Instead of focusing on hard-to-measure goals, such as student personal development, the priority became centred on measurable factors, predominantly literacy and numeracy. The need for schools to demonstrate improvement is evidenced in how the HRSB's motto changed under Olsen's tenure. When she first took the reins, her motto was that "Every student can learn. Every school can improve." It wasn't long before the word "can" was replaced with a much more imperative "will" in regards to school improvement.

Olsen's championing of data was indicative of how regional dialogue around public education was changing to reflect the global reformist idea, namely, that schools needed to improve, and they would need data to prove they were doing so. The parallels between these ideas and some of the tenets of *No Child Left Behind* were hard to ignore. As well, much of the recurring demand for school accountability could be traced directly back to the *Horizons* report, which had portrayed Nova Scotians as wanting an education system that was focused on "excellence and standards, equity and relevance."[23] That document was one of the first times that the government called for establishing "measurable standards," the achievement of which would be made publicly available in order to ensure results were realized.

That these changes were, and indeed still are, part of an evolution of the neoliberal vision for public education is evidenced in the way the recommendations from *Horizons* are remarkably similar to more modern educational reform documents. Much like the 2018 report on Nova Scotia schools, *Raise the Bar* by Dr. Avis Glaze, the impetus of the earlier document was to propose changes in school governance. Many of the same criticisms of what has commonly become known as the Glaze report appeared in policy documents of the 1990s. According to Rogers:

> *In terms of the purpose of Restructuring (1994), which was to propose changes in provincial school governance, the information provided on the "goals of education" (p 9), "the learning environment" (p 13), and the "forces of change" (p 7), at the beginning of the document did not necessarily connect to discussions of governance as seen later in the text.*[24]

As much as the discussion of the education system in the 1990s began to focus on the need for students to compete globally and was dominated by ever-increasing calls for accountability, there was also a very targeted framing during this period on "the student as the client" model. *Restructuring* referred to schools as developing into "service hubs." A model of education based on business practice was well on the way to being established.[25]

In 2002, a government strategy document called *Learning for Life: Planning for Success* (the predecessor to *Learning for Life II*) was released, which proposed that schools create a key focus on math and literacy.[26]

This objective, already being championed by the standardized testing movement, took hold rather quickly. The document makes a clear connection between overall school success and success in these core subjects. The result was more time in the school day being dedicated to teaching math, and more time and funding being allocated for professional development in the subject. The same held true for English courses, with more time, resources and testing being allocated to them.[27]

At this time policy documents began to connect student achievement with "quality teaching," and much of the language used in the early 2000s links these two things. If the tests were the measure of learning excellence, then they should also be a measure of teaching excellence. Schools were asked to produce improvement plans based on data, *à la* Carole Olsen, with a direct connection to test scores. According to Rogers, "[Nova Scotia] school improvement was directly integrated into an evidenced plan that took into account test scores . . . therefore making testing a central tenet in the accountability plan for achievement."[28]

As a further indicator of how accountability measures were creeping into the conversation, *Learning for Life* was the first document to include Nova Scotia's PISA results as a way to emphasize the need for more stringent monitoring of student success. Indeed, by 2003, a new Education Renewal Office was created within the Department of Education which was responsible for tracking "quality, standards and accountability in public schools" and ensuring they were reported upon.[29]

By 2005, the government was calling for more accountability measures to be implemented into schools, and it is here that we see the widespread promotion of the "teacher as data collector" model. As schools became more closely tied to school-wide improvement plans, and as these plans became more closely tied to standardized test scores, the need for data grew. Principals were expected to work with teachers to align their educational practice as directed by the boards and thus improve student achievement in literacy and math. The relationship between principals and teachers was changing during this time, and classroom teachers were more and more often called upon to defend their practice. No longer independent agents, teachers were expected to conform to and promote the broader goals of the Department of Education.[30]

This focus on testing and steady erosion of teacher autonomy continued for the next ten years. After the election of an NDP government in 2009, little changed in the area of public education. If anything, accountability practices increased, evidenced by the implementation of new, standardized report cards in 2010.

As expectations increased and as schools became subject to more and more accountability measures, the role of the classroom teacher changed significantly. For many teachers, time spent keeping up with accountability practices and data collection seemed to be time wasted, since many could see no connection between what they were being asked to do by the Department of Education and what they needed to do for their students. It felt for many as if their new role was to prepare students to take the tests, and they were becoming more often judged by their ability to do so. They were expected to align their own professional growth with the instructional achievement goals of the school, and, in the broader sense, the school boards and the education department. Since 2005, teachers had been asked each year to prepare professional growth plans that outlined how they were going to improve. As the impetus around data collection increased, there was a corollary demand that teachers improve in specific, measurable ways, particularly in numeracy and literacy instruction. Regardless of subject taught, teachers were expected to have goals around these two areas, and principals were expected to monitor the success of individual teachers in achieving them.

According to Rogers, this marked a major move for principals in Nova Scotia away from their traditional role as instructional leaders into a more managerial function.[31] A teacher's ability to navigate these new layers of accountability often led to increased feelings of inadequacy, which continues today. I witnessed this first-hand during a meeting I attended in 2011. A teacher stood up and spoke through tears about how she was tired of trying to decide what part of her job she was going to be bad at each day. She felt that there was no way she could meet all the demands placed upon her and still be of service to her students.

This is one of the most concerning pieces of the neoliberal puzzle and brings me back to the unknown, unintended consequences of pursuing GERM-based reform. Teachers tend, for the most part, to be rule followers. Thus, when some new piece of policy — or as has been the case lately in Nova Scotia, legislation — requires something more of them, they comply. However, what is consistently missing from the conversation is a consideration of the negative impacts these changes have on teachers, and by extension on students. Demanding that teachers collect data on school-wide literacy and numeracy goals is often framed within the overall "common sense" approach promoted by neoliberal ideology, but it comes at a price. Time spent by the drama teacher figuring out how to incorporate numeracy goals into their program comes at the cost of time spent making meaningful connections with students or planning a particularly impactful lesson.

I recognize that for some readers the damage wrought upon a school's drama program by neoliberal doctrine may not be much cause for concern. However, there is a more obvious ongoing example of how the neoliberal reforms that have crept into Nova Scotia schools have resulted in a narrowing of focus in our classrooms.

The Testing Imperative: Classroom Impacts of Data-Driven Reform

In the early 2000s, just as PISA was emerging as an educational behemoth, the Atlantic Provinces Education Foundation (APEF) was well on its way to standardizing curricula across the region. One of the major hallmarks of this effort was a push to create standardized exams for each of the areas covered by the new APEF standardized curriculum. As the new millennium dawned, the first of what would become a series of Grade 12 English exams was given to Nova Scotian students.

The English curriculum development of Atlantic Provinces Education Foundation was heavily influenced by classroom teachers, and the same was true of the exam. This assessment tool was created by a committee of classroom teachers and representatives from English Program Services, a branch of the Department of Education and Early Childhood Development. This small group of teachers and former teachers chose the texts, developed the questions and created answer keys for the exam. With a further nod to the importance of classroom teacher input, a small sample of exams were marked for a second time by a group of teachers from across the province to ensure consistency. If there was a "good way" to standardize education, this was an excellent example. However the problems and pitfalls of high-stakes standardized testing soon became apparent, and remain a concern.

The original exam format saw students assigned both reading and writing tasks, with each section accounting for 50 per cent of the overall exam mark. The exam itself was worth a full 30 per cent of the students' final Grade 12 English marks and thus had significant repercussions for their academic standing.

The reading portion of the exam always included selections of poetry, non-fiction articles, short stories and media texts such as magazine advertisements. The writing section always asked students to create an essay based on a topic given in the exam, and a persuasive writing piece, usually a letter. The exam was to be written over the course of three-and-a-half hours and, in the early days, time limits were strictly enforced. This time frame, the various weightings of the sections and the numbers of each type of reading would vary from year to year, but an overall focus on deconstructing texts and writing persuasive pieces remained.

Once it was introduced, the exam created an almost immediate change in English teaching across Nova Scotia. Since the students were measured on how well they could deconstruct poetry, non-fiction articles, short-stories and media texts, teachers across the province adapted their courses accordingly. English 12 students found themselves spending hours poring over magazine advertisements, determining why a certain colour may have been used or why a word was placed in a certain spot on the page, as opposed to, say, the ethics of advertising in general. Short-story units became a deconstructionist's dream, where examining the broader ideas of theme often took a back seat to looking at such structural considerations as why an author's word choice was particularly effective. A similar approach was brought to bear when looking at works of non-fiction, where a piece on global warming would elicit a class discussion, not on the impact of a local coal mine, but on why "When We Wrap the World in Wool" was an effective title for such an article, with a particular focus on the repeated use of the letter "w."

Of course teachers were still creating interesting units within their classrooms, but when it came to determining what to teach, the exam became a major deciding factor. Teachers knew that any work of literature they brought into the classroom, over which they did exercise some professional autonomy, must be looked at through a standardized lens. Before long, teachers began mirroring the language of the exam questions in their own classroom-based assessment, not because they believed it valuable, but to ensure students had a chance to practice. This was not only encouraged, but became a professional expectation, which, considering the exam was worth 30 per cent of a student's Grade 12 mark, was understandable. Past exams were valuable, not for their exceptionally engaging content, but for their capacity to be used as "trial runs" in order to expose students to the experience of writing a standardized examination.

This change was not limited to Grade 12 classrooms, but trickled down into Grade 11 and even into Grade 10, where teachers began mirroring what would be "expected" of students in Grade 12. As teachers began to require students to deconstruct texts as per the exam, a similar trend emerged in student writing, where focus was placed on persuasive texts and essays as opposed to writing a piece of creative satire or developing a classroom newspaper, for example. In many ways, creative writing, once such a valuable part of the English program, took a back seat to the more structured, and thus more easily evaluated, three-point essay.

Another area that suffered with the advent of the exam was that of speaking and listening, one of the three major strands of the English language arts curriculum. (The other two are writing and representing, and reading and viewing.) Traditional in-class presentations and speeches became much less common in the upper grades as more and more teachers felt pressure to prepare their students to write that all-important final exam.

There was also, as is often the case with standardized evaluation tools, a significant issue around the cultural relevance of questions in the exam. An incident from my experience in administering the exam to Grade 12 students on the Eskasoni First Nation stands out. One year, the exam contained a short story about a relationship between a child and her father. The two were at a park when a pair of deer burst out of the forest and ran across a field. One of the deer failed to make the leap over a fence that bordered the area and the Department of Natural Resources had to be called to put the animal down. Although the story was meant to elicit sympathy in the reader, many of my Mi'kmaw students were unable to see the event as anything other than a logical conclusion to the events as they had unfolded. This cultural disconnect caused my students to answer several of the questions attached to the text "incorrectly." There would be similar instances in culturally diverse classrooms across our province. And the stakes were high since Grade 12 English marks are often considered in university admissions and in the competition for academic scholarships.

Although not directly tied to teacher evaluation or performance, poor student marks could, and did, result in much more scrutiny being applied to individual classroom teachers. The message was clear: If your students did not do well in the exam, you could be called to answer for the results.

Even in the "kinder and gentler" implementation of standardized curriculum and testing that has been the reality in Nova Scotia for the past two decades, there has been an impact on classrooms and, by extension, on students. Enriching experiences such as creative writing and making speeches have certainly not completely disappeared from the in-school experience, but they have suffered from a certain lack of emphasis in a system that had become dominated by exam-based teaching and learning.

I must admit that, during this time, I was one of the converted. I attended marking sessions, changed my teaching focus and, at one point in my career, was selected by the province to develop the exam. And it must be said that there were benefits to be enjoyed by the structure that was provided in having such a common assessment. As Hargreaves argued, the result of the standardized exam was "clearer focus and greater consistency" across the province as far as English programming was concerned. Many teachers, myself included, enjoyed the structure the exam provided, and, found it possible to still create rich learning experiences for our students. However, I am also keenly aware that my practice did change when the exam was introduced, and that a great deal of my own teaching became, by necessity, focused upon my students writing it successfully. If my job had depended upon my students' marks, the level to which that focus was emphasized would have undoubtedly increased exponentially.

Since the exams have been around for almost twenty years now, in one form or another, most secondary English teachers in Nova Scotia probably don't remember teaching without them. That they have had an impact, however, is undeniable, and that they are part of a much broader movement is also a fact. It is much easier to call for an increased emphasis on standardized test scores if testing is already part of the overall educational culture of a region. At the time of writing, the exam is given to students in Grade 10 and continues to have a major impact on the English language arts curriculum. In a great many ways, the policy documents from the 1990s and early 2000s continue to drive how we are educating students in our modern classrooms.

***

Outside of Rogers's work, the impact of "neoliberal creep" upon provincial educational policy has received little serious attention. The impact on classroom teachers and students has had even less examination. Rogers describes the clear timeline of how neoliberal practices of standardization, testing and accountability have come to dominate public education in the province. She also provides evidence of the slow, incremental erosion of the teaching profession as a whole. While these various measures were implemented, teachers saw their autonomy reduced and their workload increased in ways that did not, in many instances, make much sense to them.

As teachers dealt with these added pressures (and, not insignificantly, the ever-changing challenges of the modern classroom), another outside influence was gaining momentum. In the midst of changes that so closely reflected GERM, a new organization emerged on the Nova Scotian educational landscape that would actively and aggressively promote the neoliberal ideology. Through this time of top-down change, one group led the charge to trumpet the values of competition and privatization, all the while attempting to undermine public support for both public education and struggling teachers.

CHAPTER 5
The Think Tank Campaign to Privatize

Though not all tenets of neoliberalism have been adopted in Nova Scotia, many of those ideas have become firmly entrenched in the discussions and policies surrounding education. Increased focus on standardized testing, teacher accountability, focus on competitiveness; more and more, the ideology is alive and well in our province.

To expand on Sahlberg's discussion of GERM, ideologies, much like viruses, need hosts to spread them. In Canada, the promotion mechanism for GERM has been privately funded, well-resourced think tanks. A number of these institutions have a long history of promoting a neoliberal perspective on everything from economics to education. The best-known of the Canadian think tanks is the Vancouver-based Fraser Institute. Founded in 1974, it is one of Canada's largest independent think tanks, with offices in Calgary, Montreal, Toronto and Vancouver. It promotes itself with the altruistic claim in its mission statement that it exists to "improve the quality of life for Canadians."[1] The Fraser Institute has long had a major interest in public education, often focusing on what it considers overspending, and consistently uses standardized test results to promote its claims.

In Nova Scotia, the Atlantic Institute for Market Studies (AIMS) operated for over two decades until it merged with the Fraser Institute in November 2019. Although AIMS was small in size, it had a significant impact upon current educational policy.

Founded in 1994, AIMS quickly established itself as a voice of free-ranging capitalism in Atlantic Canada. One of its earliest publications was the 1996 book *Looking the Gift Horse in the Mouth: The Impact of Federal Transfers on Atlantic Canada*. Written by AIMS senior policy analyst Fred McMahon, the book aligned itself with pro-free-market views, including trumpeting the values of the free market and criticizing unionized labour.[2]

From the beginning, AIMS was supported by many wealthy business people from the Atlantic Provinces, many of whom were under the impression that they had the capacity to improve systems they knew little about by virtue of their bank accounts. One of its earliest benefactors was millionaire Purdy Crawford, and in 2019 the AIMS board of governors included such corporate heavyweights as McCain Foods' Scott McCain, Corporate Research Associates founder Don Mills and John Risley of seafood industry giant Clearwater.[3]

John Risley reportedly began his career selling lobster out of the back of a truck. He now owns one of the most successful business enterprises in Canada. With a net worth of $1.2 billion in 2019, Risley has been a major AIMS benefactor for a number of years and is a staunch believer in the tenets of neoliberalism. On the AIMS website, Risley spelled out his vision for the organization:

> Let me assure you that AIMS will continue to be the voice of sensible policy in our region; to hold government accountable for its size and activities; to be better at what it needs to be good at and to step aside from those activities that are best left to the private sector and market forces.[4]

One of the activities to which Risley refers is education. In a 2013 article in *Atlantic Business Magazine*, he declared "we have the worst P–12 education system in the country. That's not subjective. We have the worst goddamn math scores in the country!"[5] (We don't, by the way.) Regardless, it was clear by this, and subsequent declarations of a similar ilk, what he believed about our public schools.

Not only is Risley a staunch neoliberal (and very wealthy), he also has significant political influence. The lines of connectivity are impressive. For example, in August 2016 it was reported that Risley had been chosen by Dalhousie University as one of a group of business elites from Nova Scotia to attend a prestigious international conference at Massachusetts Institute of Technology (MIT), the cost of which was borne by the university.[6] Considering his net financial worth, this "free ride" raised a few eyebrows, particularly since tuition rates at Dalhousie were on the rise.

When asked about the decision, Premier Stephen McNeil, who has embarked on several trade missions to China in order to open markets for the Nova Scotian seafood industry, defended the university's decision, calling the event "an amazing link." The university also defended the move, claiming that they were hoping to recoup expenses through fundraising efforts. The trip was overseen by Dalhousie University president Richard Florizone, also a member of the AIMS board of directors at the time.

Dalhousie's gamble paid off when, in September of 2016, Risley donated $25 million to the university to fund ocean research.

The close ties between industry, government and the upper echelons of academia to the neoliberal movement leave little wonder as to why the ideology has proliferated. However, Risley is only one of the organization's supporters. Former AIMS chair John Irving's family fortune is approximately $7 billion. The McCain empire is valued in excess of $4.5 billion. Lee Bragg, another member of the board, operates the Eastlink corporation, worth around $1.3 billion. I can think of no other organization in Atlantic Canada that has been supported by such an extensive amount of individual and corporate influence.

From its very beginning, AIMS was interested in seeing the public-education system overhauled, dedicating some of its earliest forays into the field of public-sector criticism to campaigns around such ideas as school choice, echoing the ideas of Milton Friedman. In order to understand what AIMS is promoting, it is worth taking a moment to explain what is meant by "school choice" and why so many with an interest in preserving public education consider it a threat.

Groups such as AIMS and the Fraser Institute believe that free-market theory should apply to a wide variety of public-sector institutions, including schools. The idea is that consumers of education should be able to compare schools on the basis of course offerings and test scores, teaching methods or philosophies of thought, and then choose the school that best suits their own child's needs. In neoliberal ideology, if a competitive market does not exist in a field like education, then it is the responsibility of the government to create the conditions under which one can be established.

This reality of offering students and parents choice in public schools would be challenging in Nova Scotia. In many parts of the province, the population can barely support one public school, let alone multiple ones. (Friedman addresses this issue by allowing for the establishing of school choice in areas where it can be sustained.) The idea of school choice, however, is not necessarily about comparing one public school to another, but a way of comparing public schools to alternative choices. Thus, the phrase "school choice" is often closely connected to another neo-liberal construct, the charter school.

A charter school is one set up by a non-governmental organization to offer an educational program that differs in some way from the regular public system. A charter school can be started by any group of stakeholders who get together and decide they can do a better, more customized job of educating students than the public system. In some cases, these stakeholders are people from the community, or, perhaps, a group of concerned parents who share a common interest or philosophy. They can also, however, be private for-profit companies that have a vested interest in accessing public-sector dollars. Regardless of the source of funding, in order to set up a school, the group must create a charter statement. Charter statements lay out what curriculum a school will offer, how students will be assessed, where money will be spent and which students will be served. Charter schools are usually licensed by some kind of regulatory body, which is expected to hold the school accountable for meeting the terms of its charter.

Charter schools have had mixed results, particularly in the United States, where they have been promoted for years and have been a particular focus of Donald Trump's billionaire education secretary Betsy DeVos since she was given the office.[7] In 2017, an organization called the Network for Public Education evaluated the charter model as a "waste of millions of taxpayer dollars."[8] One-time assistant director of education under George W. Bush and key architect of the *No Child Left Behind* reform, Diane Ravitch, has characterized the charter-school movement in that country as being an absolute and abject disaster. An online search of "charter school failure" reveals dozens of stories of failed schools across the United States.

There are, of course, charter-school success claims. A 2013 report from a group called the Center for Research on Education Outcomes concluded that charter schools in the US were actually improving student ability in areas such as reading.[9] However, only a few years before, a major study done for the US Department of Education was unable to find any significant benefit that charters had over regular public schools.[10]

The only jurisdiction in Canada that allows charter schools is Alberta, where they are very tightly monitored and regulated. They were first adopted during the neoliberal explosion of the early nineties, and Alberta has legislation that lays out clear expectations for these schools and ensures that they adhere closely to provincial standards. Much like their American cousins, Canadian charter movements have met resistance from a number of groups, most notably teacher organizations. From the British Columbia Teachers Federation to the Nova Scotia Teachers Union, public educators have been almost unanimous in their condemnation of the model.

One common criticism of charter schools is that they draw funding away from the public system. Most jurisdictions, including Nova Scotia, fund schools on a per-student basis. Thus, the more students you have, the more money you get. When a charter school is opened, they are funded in a similar way, so that the school receives a grant from the governing educational body equivalent to what a public school would have received for those students, as per Friedman's model. Thus, when the new charter school opens, the students who leave the public school take their government funding with them, and the amount of public monies available to the public system for offering programs and supporting students is reduced.

Another criticism of charter schools is based on social justice and equality. Although charter schools may not actually provide a "better" education, there may be a perception among parents that they will. If parents have become convinced that the public system is failing (driven by think-tank-created Fear, Uncertainty and Doubt), the charter school across town may seem especially attractive. However, there is a certain level of financial stability required to be able to get children to the school each morning. For some, dropping a minivan-load of learners off at a charter school door each day is a straightforward feat; for others, a financial or logistical impossibility. As well, parents with socio-economic advantages such as a higher level of education or income tend to be more engaged. When they leave the neighbourhood school in favour of the charter across town, their advocacy skills go with them. Thus, not only does the neighbourhood public school lose the potential benefits of having these champions working in their favour, they face the daunting task of having to compete against their more outspoken, cross-town competition for ever-shrinking resources.

The fear of the anti-charter movement is that this becomes a vicious cycle. Parents who have the financial means (and the capacity to navigate complicated bureaucracies) will remove their children from the regular public-school system and send them to charter schools. As funding and advocacy decrease, so too does the public school's ability to access resources for its remaining students. Without appropriate resources, the school continues to decline and becomes even less attractive. Eventually, the public school becomes financially nonviable and ultimately closes, leaving the charter school as the only option available to parents. At its logical conclusion, the introduction of charter schools can see control of public education move outside of the public realm.

This alone is enough to cause the more socially minded to object to the charter-school model. In Nova Scotia, as in many jurisdictions across the country, students are being denied resources due to funding restraints. You need only visit your local elementary school to see the wide variety of needs and wants that exist in the modern classroom. Imagine if two students (and their associated funding) were removed from each class in that school because their parents determined they should attend the cross-town charter. Losing two students in each class would not allow for staff reductions, or fewer janitors, or lower the number of buses required. The only thing that would be reduced would be funding for the school itself. Cuts would need to be made, but the only place where that could happen would be in services. There would be fewer dollars for student supports, for sports teams, for breakfast programs — so many of the vital elements that make public school such a positive public resource would be lost in the name of competition and free markets.

While the deterioration of the local public school may be of some concern in itself, there is an even more disturbing element to the charter-school movement. While most of us think about public education working for the common good, this is in fundamental conflict with the neoliberal worldview. When the public education system is controlled by the private sector, education becomes a for-profit enterprise — an enterprise focused on making good profits, not good people.

In the US, the increased demand for charter schools has closely paralleled the rise of companies that seek to operate them for a profit. Possibly the best known is the Knowledge Is Power Program (KIPP), a non-profit group that has opened over two hundred charter schools since its inception in 1994. Although there have been some very successful KIPP schools, there has been an almost constant push back against these Educational Management Organizations (EMOs) from public education activists. One of the key objections is that many of the non-profit organizations in the charter-school movement are backed by major business interests. The Knowledge is Power Program itself was backed by Donald Fisher, one of the co-founders of the clothing brand GAP.[11] This leads to an entirely new kind of business where educationally focused enterprises are run by very well-paid executives, many of whom have a business background as opposed to an educational one. For example, although listed as a not-for-profit, KIPP paid out in excess of US$1.4 million in salaries to its top brass in 2017, with its CEO earning approximately US$300,000.[12] Although it may be argued that Mr. Fisher gets to spend his wealth how he sees fit, the rest of us might look at these managerial salaries and consider how much good the money could do at the classroom level.

The promotion of school choice and charter schools has led to several US jurisdictions becoming almost completely privatized. The results of this trend have been unimpressive. For example, a 2017 *New York Times* article reported that when it came to improving student achievement, Betsy DeVos's home state of Michigan placed dead last in the US.[13] The state also has more charter schools than any other state in the country, with upwards of 80 per cent of schools there run as for-profit enterprises.

Not only has the private charter-school movement in the US been plagued by stories of student failure, it has been the source of countless incidents of fraud and corruption. In fact, the Network for Public Education has taken to Twitter using the hashtag #anotherdayanothercharterscandal to track the pervasiveness of this trend.[14] The NPE has documented dozens of these stories, which often involve real-estate wheeling and dealing.

One common scam works as follows. An organization, often a not-for-profit, is granted permission to open a charter school. They rent a building from a real-estate company using the state-provided per-student funding. The real money comes into play when the building owner charges the not-for-profit well-above-market rental fees. In some instances, the not-for-profit itself was originally established and funded by the owners of the real-estate company. Thus, tax payers' money is channelled away from the students, and directly into the pockets of the wealthy real-estate owners.

The potential for profit making from public education has produced another effect in the US. In many jurisdictions where the public system has withstood the charter-school movement, private interests have attempted to influence the legislative process by using not-for-profit enterprises to back pro-charter political candidates. This effort has happened at the higher levels of the democratic process, but also at the level of local school boards. In a 2017 article in the *Washington Post*, advocates Carol Burris and Darcie Simarusti showed how wealthy business people were pouring millions of dollars into local school-board elections in order to elect supporters of charter schools.[15] This funding model is often referred to as "dark money" and has become widespread in the US, and inspired a 2018 PBS documentary on the subject.[16]

As the role of private business interests in the public education system has increased, so too has the debate around the wisdom of the idea. To give a sense of the breadth of the discussion, the National Center for the Study of Privatization in Education at Columbia University alone has, since its inception in 2000, published dozens of papers on the intricacies of the trend and has generated five books on the subject.[17]

Having a hulking neighbour to the south can be both a blessing and a curse in that, as much as we often inherit their sometimes dubious trends, we also can avail ourselves of their research. Since Canada has just one province that allows charter schools, and does so in a manner that is different from the US model, we are limited in our ability to judge the relative success or failure of the movement here, and so I reference the American experience as a cautionary tale. Although Canadians like to envision themselves as being very different from Americans, the ideology driving educational trends on both sides of the border is remarkably similar. As the push for the adoption of more free-market thinking in our schools grows, so too does the potential for us to follow in American footsteps. It is of some note that the recently elected Alberta premier, Jason Kenney, included an expansion of charter schools as one of his key election promises. (Kenney was the keynote speaker at the AIMS Chairman's Dinner in 2018, an event sponsored by John Risley.) Although the neoliberal view of education would see increased competition as a means to achieving better results, three decades of increasingly neoliberal educational reform in the United States have simply not delivered. There is no evidence that shows charter schools have improved the American education system, and plenty of evidence that points to individual profits, not school improvement, being the major motivator.

AIMS has been a long-standing and vocal champion of creating a competitive model of education in Atlantic Canada, particularly with regards to school choice and charter schools. And, as the whole premise of charter schools is one of competition, it makes sense that an organization dedicated to advancing the cause of free-market thinking should be so aligned. As early as 1997, the organization proposed that charter schools could be a solution for a system they determined was "lagging behind" the rest of the country. One of their earliest position publications on the subject, *Charter Schools in Atlantic Canada: An Idea Whose Time Has Come* by Joe Freedman (assisted by Fred McMahon), used the following passage by Ted Kolderie, from the now-renamed Center for Policy Studies in Saint Paul, Minnesota, to summarize their vision:

> *The essential idea is worth restating: It is to offer change-oriented educators or others the opportunity to go either to the local school board or to some other public body for a contract under which they would set up an autonomous (and therefore performance-based) public school which students could choose to attend without charge.*[18]

The book offered several key arguments as to why it was vital at the time to enact these changes, citing "intense international economic competition" and lagging academic achievement. Celebrating the idea of school deregulation as a key component to success, *Charter Schools* encouraged Atlantic Canada to adopt a system that was less restrictive than the one Alberta had adopted a few years before, determining that, unlike Alberta, there should be no cap on the number of charter schools permitted to open. As well, it was quite concerned about allowing what it called "boutique" schools to gain the "lion's share" of the charters, should they be approved. These boutique schools were classed as those schools that might serve only certain types of students — in their own words, such students as "disaffected teenagers, the handicapped, etc."[19] AIMS felt that too many of the available charters in Alberta had gone to servicing this "type" of student.

Another book by Joe Freedman, entitled *Charter Schools in Ontario: An Idea Whose Time Has Come*, was released in 1996. It would seem that a simple jurisdictional name change allows for a certain universal application of neoliberal ideas, at least as far as the neoliberals are concerned.

It is worth re-stating that the charter-school model, when adopted in its purest form, allows for private companies to profit from public education. The cost to the taxpayer does not decrease. The per student funding as determined by the government does not go down when charter schools are introduced into a system; the money simply goes to a private entity, rather than a public one.

Over the years, AIMS has produced a wide variety of position papers on other educational issues, and continued to increase their emphasis on school competition and standardized testing. In 2003, they released their first annual "report card" for high schools in Nova Scotia, through which schools were graded based on AIMS's own criteria. This report card, which mirrored similar efforts from the Fraser Institute, became a staple of the AIMS organization and was published in an effort to increase the public appetite for more comparison among schools. The organization also continued to display an infatuation with the Alberta education system, hosting events where such charter-school champions as Angus McBeath, former superintendent of Edmonton's public-school system, spoke about the virtues of school choice. Around the same time, the views of Rodney Clifton, who was then a professor of sociology at the University of Manitoba, also began to gain prominence with AIMS.

Importing experts from outside of the Atlantic Provinces to comment on the region's education system has become somewhat of a trademark for the organization. In 2007, they engaged Clifton to work with Michael Zwaagstra, a high-school teacher from Manitoba who had produced reports for Frontier Center for Public Policy of Winnipeg (another Atlas Network partner), and John C. Long from the University of Calgary's School of Public Policy, which has close ties with neoliberal think-tank ideology and "Big Oil."[20] That the authors used by AIMS are almost invariably neither from Nova Scotia nor employed in the region's public education system is worth noting.

The 2007 paper that was produced by this collaboration was important for a number of reasons. Although often critical of the public-school system, the entire thrust of the 2007 AIMS paper *Getting the Fox out of the Schoolhouse: How the Public Can Take Back Public Education* was that when it came to true and meaningful reform, it was teacher organizations, specifically unions, that were standing in the way.[21]

Getting the Fox out of the Schoolhouse identified several concerns about the role that unions played in schools, which it framed as working against the best interests of students, parents and taxpayers. The paper criticized these organizations for resisting the trends around standardization, performance-based pay for teachers and the charter-school movement, and for thus inhibiting "the development of effective schools."[22] That union resistance to these neoliberal ideologies served any sort of greater good was dismissed and framed as self-serving, echoing strongly the teachings of Friedman and Hayek.

It is worth pointing out the similar tone toward education that was adopted by the Nova Scotia government a few years later. This is most evident in the way in which the paper framed school principals as managers who were not as effective as they could be due to union affiliation. In it, AIMS complained that since "school administrators, who are supposed to function as on-site managers, are themselves former teachers and are both more sympathetic to teachers' values and expectations" they were "less attached to their role as managers who must also represent the interests of the employer, parents, and taxpayers."[23] Further, AIMS complained that "such a situation places principals in a conflict of interest, constraining their ability to perform the classical managerial functions of planning, leadership, organization, and evaluation on behalf of their employer," phrasing that echoes the language ultimately used to remove principals from the Nova Scotia Teachers Union in 2018.

This scathing review of the system in Nova Scotia was coming from two individuals who had no evidence or experience that the current system was in any way "constraining." They provided no examples where this supposed conflict of interest had been a problem in a school, no reports of situations where principals had not represented "the interests of the employer, parents and taxpayers" and no research that supported their claim that this model, even if adopted, would result in any sort of improvement. Framing their argument in the typical "common-sense" rhetoric of the neoliberals, and then using that argument to create Fear, Uncertainty and Doubt, was how they advanced their position.

There were five key recommendations highlighted in *Getting the Fox out of the Schoolhouse* to improve the education system. That they sound familiar to anyone following the educational unrest of 2015–18 indicates the level to which this thinking permeated the highest ranks of government. The report recommended:

- Provincial and territorial governments should use and continue to refine a standardized testing regime to assess the achievement of students on provincial curricula, especially in language, mathematics and science.

- Provincial governments should give parents a greater choice of schools to which they may send their children, primarily in recognition of the diversity of interests and expectations parents have concerning their children's education.

- Provincial governments and school boards should consider how teachers' compensation schemes could be adjusted so that salary increments are dependent on performance and outstanding teachers and schools are recognized more effectively.

- In the interests of managing schools more effectively, principals should be removed from the bargaining unit for teachers.

- Strikes and lockouts should no longer be permitted as ways of resolving disputes in public-school systems.[24]

The paper received a fair amount of media attention, and essentially encapsulated the neoliberal agenda. The call for more standardized testing, more school choice, merit-based pay for teachers and, perhaps most significantly, an attack on collective bargaining all positioned AIMS as fundamentally neoliberal and one of the "secondhand dealers in ideas" that Hayek had envisioned back in the 1940s. The pervasiveness of the AIMS message and the extent to which they were successful in spreading their thinking would not become fully evident until 2018, but this paper would turn out to be a sign of things to come.

In order to enact a new system, you have to first convince those in power that the system needs replacing. When it comes to questioning the value and effectiveness of public education, and encouraging Unsupported Deficiency Syndrome, AIMS has been a textbook example of how such groups, with a frustrating tenacity, can influence public understanding and attitudes.

The next chapter examines how, over the course of a relatively short period of time, public perception of education and of the teaching profession shifted. As we moved into the second decade of the twenty-first century, the narrative of how effective our system was at educating our children became more and more closely scrutinized. As technologies changed and classrooms became more transparent, teachers and indeed the very craft of teaching were exposed like never before. This was an exciting but also challenging time to be an educator. New technologies were being introduced at a rapid pace, and the development of the Internet opened up tremendous opportunities for learning. At the same time, pressures increased for more accountability and individualization of instruction, as well as for more data and measurement.

Against this high-pressure backdrop, humming just under the surface and gaining ground, was the notion that our schools were failing. And before long, Nova Scotia was suffering from a full-blown case of Unsupported Deficiency Syndrome, with the condition being exacerbated by AIMS and helped along by a seemingly complicit media that seemed to have an insatiable appetite for this particular brand of "the sky is falling" rhetoric.

CHAPTER 6
How the Media Turned Nova Scotia Against Its Teachers (2010–2014)

When the teachers and the government of Nova Scotia were locked in the throes of the 2015–18 disputes, one of the key questions being asked by parents and the public in general was why teachers seemed so darn angry.

It is worth reiterating that during this period there had been several new initiatives launched that were seeing more and more demands being made of teachers' time. These included an increase in the expectations around the collection and collation of data to satisfy school improvement goals; the introduction of a new online grading system that gave parents and students access to teachers' marking systems in real time; and changes to the ways in which report-card comments were expected to be written. Each of these initiatives were created to satisfy the increasing pressure for "school accountability," and each became another task that took teacher focus away from what they often saw as more important work.

Looking from the top down, many of these initiatives made sense. For instance, the collection of data was promoted as a way for schools to determine where they were on the learning continuum and where they needed to go. Without large-scale data garnered from board-wide standardized tests, how could schools know if their efforts were having an impact? Parents were framed as being partners in the learning of their children, so they should be able to go online as they wished to see where their child stood academically. Finally, since parents were having a difficult time understanding what report card comments were saying about their child's learning, and since the report card was a key conduit of communication between the school and home, it made sense to standardize so that communication was clear.

As is often the case, the view from the top is very different than the view from the bottom. When it came to data collection and collation, teachers often found that they did not understand what they were collecting, or even, in many cases, why. It became common for schools to develop literacy and numeracy improvement goals, and the achievement of these goals was meant to permeate every facet of the curriculum. As already noted, teachers were expected to include a connection to these goals in their own professional growth plans — a document produced each year by teachers to explain how they themselves planned on improving. I can tell you that, as a high-school English and drama teacher, making numeracy a major focus of my professional growth was challenging to say the least.

It was a similar situation with the introduction of online grade books. Although throwing open the doors of a teacher's marking scheme certainly offered a modicum of reassurance to those who desired more accountability, in practice, things were very different. Teachers sometimes found themselves spending precious time explaining how the marking system worked to the helicopter parents among us, at the expense of other more valuable duties.

Report cards also became a bone of contention. In 2013, *The Chronicle Herald* published a piece called "Parents Weary of Report Card 'Mumbo Jumbo.'"[1] It attacked jargon-filled report cards whose comments on student achievement left parents baffled. The next day, CBC Nova Scotia ran a piece on how parents were confused by the comments that were written on their student's report cards and how this complaint was widespread.[2] Criticism in the media was followed the next day, July 4, by an announcement from the minister of education that she would be looking at the way report cards were written, and the process was ultimately changed.

This may seem fairly mundane, particularly to those who have never had to write a report card. However, the way report cards were being created by teachers at the time of the complaints had already been mandated. Just a few years before, teachers had been instructed to use a standardized reporting system. Teachers had complained then that the new system was clunky and made little sense, but their complaints were largely ignored.

The result of the 2013 story was that teachers were made to follow yet another different standardized template for report card comments. Many of them had spent considerable time adjusting to the previous changes and now needed to start again because the issue had made the six o'clock news. This was only one example of the new frustrations teachers were experiencing.

Mixed in to all this was the added confusion of "no-zero" policies, "no-fail" policies and weak, if even existent, attendance policies. At a time when accountability practices were being ratcheted up for teachers, it seemed that the opposite was true for students. Conversations around students not submitting work became less and less about what the *student* was not doing and became more and more about what the *teacher* was not doing. Each of these changes may have, individually, emerged from sound rationale, but they were having a major cumulative effect. What was perhaps even more challenging was the extent to which these changes were being driven by public pressure as opposed to sound educational policy.

This is how, when it comes to the advent of GERM and, more particularly, the onset of Unsupported Deficiency Syndrome, the media plays a pivotal role. If the reformists can get their FUD message out consistently through the media, then their narrative stops being just opinion and becomes part of a collectively understood truth. If it is stated often enough that things are not going well in public schools, pretty soon that becomes a universal understanding. This understanding, regardless of its validity, often results in action from politicians. This is the exact state of affairs envisioned by Hayek when he spoke of secondhand dealers in ideas — individuals who were not necessarily experts in a field nor in possession of any special knowledge on a subject. All that was needed was to be readily able to speak or write on a topic, possessing just enough information to sound authoritative to the average person.

Keeping in mind that things in the classroom were in a constant state of flux, and that there was already evidence that government policy could be misinformed by media hype, three stories had a tremendous impact on the events of 2015–18. These stories give a sense of the climate of the time: a climate in which teachers were clearly portrayed as being substandard and, in some cases, dishonest, and where the system was being framed as abjectly failing our students.

Professional Upgrades

In February 2014, just as the new Liberal government was working on legislating an end to a labour dispute with health workers, CBC reporter Bob Murphy broke a story about how some teachers in Nova Scotia were taking advantage of online courses that were being offered by Drake University in Des Moines, Iowa, in order to achieve professional licence upgrades.[3]

For context, it is useful to know that teachers in Nova Scotia are paid on a salary scale that depends on their years of experience and their qualifications. Once teachers achieve a permanent contract, they receive automatic pay increases for the first decade of their careers, each worth about $2,800 or so per year. When it comes to qualifications, teachers can take degree or diploma programs through accredited post-secondary institutions to achieve credential upgrades. Some of these programs consist of traditional classroom set-ups; some, like Drake University, are offered digitally; and some are a combination of the two. Before beginning any program, teachers must first apply and receive approval from the Department of Education. Upon completion, teachers can expect a pay increase of anywhere between $8,700 per year for their first upgrade, to about $5,000 for their third and final one.

The CBC report presented this upgrade as a sordid tale of how teachers were, in effect, milking the system by taking the distance education courses from Drake University. At the heart of the piece was the suggestion that this diploma — and specifically the Drake course in physical education — was not academically rigorous enough to be worthy of any increase in pay.

To comment on the quality of the cause, Murphy sought the advice of local education consultant and frequent AIMS author Dr. Paul W. Bennett. Of the Drake courses, Bennett had commented, "They are not legitimate courses and they don't meet the common standards for graduate work which they're being used as an equivalent to." Bennett accused the teachers involved of "cherry-picking" courses that he felt were minimally demanding, in order to achieve "maximum benefit."[4]

The Drake program differed from traditional university courses in that it did not require face-to-face time with university faculty, but asked teachers to complete an online curriculum and submit the completed work electronically. The program offered a tremendous amount of flexibility because it did not have any scheduled class times and allowed teachers to complete a unit of study on their own time. A teacher could dedicate, say, a week over the March Break to completing dozens of hours of coursework to complete a unit of study, without having to attend a pre-determined schedule of classes. Conversely, teachers could work at a more incremental pace. Upon completing the work teachers were given a pass or a fail — a style of marking not uncommon in post-secondary programs.

The Drake University program was attractive not only for how it was structured, but also for the content it offered. The content was applicable to physical education teachers, for whom there were very few, if any, local offerings, but also served the needs of teachers who might find themselves running a class like Healthy Living or Leadership. Although eligible to take a more traditional upgrade in areas such as "curriculum" or "administrative leadership," many found the Drake courses much more practical than other, perhaps more academically inclined, offerings. Being able to immediately apply what was learned from the Drake courses in their classrooms (or gymnasiums, as the case may be) was one of the most appealing aspects of the program for many teachers.

Finally, the price tag for the Drake courses was significantly lower than other programs, costing hundreds of dollars less per course than other upgrades. In the end, Drake offered a flexible, practical and less expensive option for teachers wishing to improve their classroom practice. It is small wonder that the institution was gaining popularity.

Bennett's background qualifying him to comment on this topic included time as a headmaster at a Halifax private school, but he had retired from that post a few years before. An import from the Ontario private-school system, he was an adjunct professor for a Halifax university, but that institution did not have a teacher-training program. Bennett had no position with the provincial Department of Education, which would have perhaps given him some authority to speak on teacher certification, nor had he ever worked in the public-school system. In short, there seemed to be little in Bennett's resume that would qualify him to provide well-informed comment.

However, Bennett actively promoted himself as an educational consultant through his business, Schoolhouse Consulting, and was an easily accessible source for commentary on educational issues. He had written a book that focused on rural education in

Nova Scotia, and had published several op-ed pieces regarding public education in a variety of media outlets. His strongest credentials stemmed from AIMS, for whom he had authored several position papers.

Once this sensational story broke, there was a huge public outcry. Even though Drake University was not particularly unique in its offering of degrees and certificates via distance education, the idea that the course material was offered via CD-ROM seemed to be a particular bone of contention for critics. When it was revealed that some of the teachers taking the program were not Physical Education teachers, there was further outcry. The comments on the original online CBC report (179 in total) were predominantly negative toward the teachers involved, with much of the criticism suggesting that teachers were being both lazy and greedy. Attempts to explain the relative value of the Drake courses as far as their applicability, their flexibility or their more affordable price tag were met with derision and scorn.

The irony regarding this controversy was that the Department of Education had pre-approved the teachers to take the course. They had all applied to the department before starting the program, as was the case for all such upgrades. If there were issues around academic rigour, you would expect that it would have been the department that would bear the brunt of the criticism. However, this key fact was lost in the melee and mayhem. The notion that teachers were rampantly abusing the licence system caught on like wildfire. In response to the media pressure, the minister of education announced that the department would be launching an investigation into the matter and looking into how teachers were certified as a whole.

A few months later, in April 2014, this issue grabbed headlines again when the minister announced that courses from Drake University would be removed from those approved to be used for teacher upgrades.[5] The minister explained that her office had reviewed the Drake offerings and had found them lacking, and that they did not "match what we believe is good intensive professional development upgrading for teachers."[6] She did, however, concede that teachers who were already enrolled in the Drake courses would be allowed to finish the program and receive an upgrade.

Once again, criticism was swift and harsh. On April 30, *Chronicle Herald* columnist Marilla Stephenson chastised the minister for not recognizing that the province was broke and bemoaned higher teacher salaries resulting from the upgrades.[7] The former CEO of Maritime Life, Bill Black, rang alarm bells about how the upgrades could cost taxpayers upwards of $60 million and spoke of how "The big cost . . . is not tuition, but rather the resulting pay increases."[8,9] In a very short space of time, the assessment of the relative value of one program of study, an assessment that had originally been offered by someone with no specific qualifications on the matter, turned into a public debate on the merit of upgrades in the first place. Suddenly, the integrity of all teachers was being questioned. The media narrative centred around the portrayal of teachers taking shortcuts to pay raises that they did not deserve and for which the public was footing the bill.

To further demonstrate the impact of the "mediafication" of public education, the issue of the Drake upgrades surfaced a third time almost a year later in a particularly bizarre way. On February 24, 2015, another public outcry was instigated when Bennett wrote an op-ed piece for *The Chronicle Herald*, decrying the number of days schools had been closed that winter due to bad weather. He once again adopted an alarmist perspective, suggesting that these closures were having a detrimental impact on student achievement. He claimed, "Cancelling school days for real or threatened severe weather . . . is only compounding our student performance challenges. No school system anywhere can be competitive when students are only in school for 165 to 175 of the scheduled 180 to 182 instructional days."[10]

Bennett provided no evidence that there was any causal connection between snow days and student achievement; however, his analysis was once again treated as having considerable validity.

He was widely interviewed on the subject, and he appeared on several local media outlets to expand on his concerns.

Snow days are certainly disruptive for parents and caregivers who are often left scrambling to find childcare when schools are closed. As had been the case with the Drake University accreditation, the conversation soon became less about the academic impact such days have on student achievement and more about how teachers were receiving another undeserved perk, in this case, a paid day off work. As the public furor mounted, Minister of Education Karen Casey was grilled about the supposed damage being done to student achievement by such closures. In response, on February 26, Casey indicated that she was considering enacting a seldom used power of the education minister to make up for such lost days by sending students to school on Saturdays or by having them attend during March Break, a declaration that made national headlines.[11] This was met with its own public outcry that resounded with as much ferocity as the closures themselves had elicited, with much of the anger being directed at the minister.

In the midst of a storm of criticism on snow days, the minister made an announcement that took everyone by surprise. On March 3, she announced that "Effective today, the department will no longer grant an increase in teacher certification to teachers who take video correspondence courses from Drake University, including teachers pre-approved to take the course."[12]

By way of defence, the minister pointed to a public-opinion survey her government had recently distributed to ask for input on the public-education system (discussed in Chapter 7). She claimed that the survey had revealed that Nova Scotians recognized "the importance of teachers being engaged in quality professional development that will benefit students," and, since the public felt the Drake courses were unworthy, the decision was justified.[13]

Let's review: Teachers who had applied to Drake had been approved for their courses by the Department of Education. Then they were accused of milking the system, mostly on the grounds of a sensationalist media piece that had been fuelled by someone associated with AIMS. Teachers were then assured they could complete their course of study by the minister of education, and many had moved forward in good faith to do just that. Suddenly this decision was reversed, with no justification other than the results of a public-opinion survey that had undoubtedly been heavily influenced by the very same sensationalist AIMS-fuelled media piece from the year before.

This abrupt about-face would eventually lead to a successful court challenge by the NSTU, a settlement which will reportedly cost Nova Scotia taxpayers $7.5 million.[14] However, as far as a device for taking the spotlight off the minister's comments on snow days, it was exceptionally effective. The general public almost immediately forgot about the idea of Saturday school days and were once again, quite skillfully, directed to focus on "those greedy teachers."

This story, and the accompanying public outcry, serves as a clear example of how public opinion was being manipulated to drive policy — policy that aligned nicely with the neoliberal ideas of more accountability practices for teachers.

If the Drake issue had been an isolated incident, the contention that sensationalist rhetoric played a major role in decision making during this time could be dismissed. But this was only one of a number of cases where there was a line from individuals who were connected to or funded by the Atlantic Institute for Market Studies to negative public perception of teachers.

Spotless Records

At the same time as the news story around teachers taking online upgrades was making headlines, AIMS released a position paper co-authored by Paul Bennett and Karen Mitchell, entitled *Maintaining "Spotless Records": Professional Standards, Teacher Misconduct and the Teaching Profession*.[15] In its executive summary, the paper started off with this warning:

> *Certifying teachers and regulating the teaching profession is emerging as a critical public policy issue — and one that urgently needs addressing in the interests of students as well as taxpayers in Nova Scotia and a few other provinces. Establishing and maintaining professional standards in Canada has, in practice, been delegated to provincial teachers' unions and federations. Nova Scotia demonstrates how that approach can be particularly loose and mostly ineffective, virtually guaranteeing "spotless records" for teachers.*[16]

One of the arguments of the paper was that the Drake issue had "revealed a serious flaw in the whole teacher regulation regime."[17] The paper called into question whether teaching could even be called a "profession" any longer, considering the extent to which teachers were now lacking accountability. The authors used slipping test scores as evidence that schools were failing, and were harshly critical of the Nova Scotia Teachers Union for having defended teachers who had taken the Drake program. They wrote of how then-president Shelley Morse had "shocked many by publicly defending the teachers' actions in finding a loophole in the provincial certification regulation system . . . How and why the NSTU leadership felt compelled to come forward to defend the inappropriate actions and cover up the union's actual role is the fundamental question raised and addressed in this AIMS research report."[18]

The paper identified an urgent need for governing bodies to establish a set of professional teaching standards and accountability practices that would ensure the quality of teachers. It repeated the sentiment, long promoted by AIMS, that the NSTU was in the business of doing everything it could to protect underperforming educators. The paradox, however, was that although the paper was touted as being research-based, its pages were littered with inaccurate information about how the Nova Scotia education system worked.

As one of its major contentions, *Spotless Records* was critical of the way in which the professional development of teachers was handled, and, specifically, the role played in that development by the Nova Scotia Teachers Union (NSTU). The authors complained that "Professional development of teachers in Nova Scotia remains the exclusive preserve of the NSTU,"[19] but this is a misleading and inaccurate statement. The NSTU co-governs (with the Department of Education) a fund that teachers can access to take such training, but has little direct influence over teacher professional development. The union provides funding and support for teachers to create professional development opportunities for their peers during one day annually in October (commonly called October Conference). Beyond that, responsibility for professional development lies primarily with the Department of Education and, more commonly, its Regional Education Centres.

A second major example of an inaccurate description of the education system was in the authors' denunciation of the existing processes for assessment and evaluation of teachers. In the document, they called for the introduction of regular teacher assessments to take place every five to seven years. They seemed not to know that teachers in Nova Scotia were required to provide proof of professional growth to their immediate supervisors on an *annual* basis. Most teachers were expected to fill out growth plans at the beginning of the year, which were read and approved by either an administrator or a department head and needed to be directly connected to their professional practice. Teachers were then expected to work toward achieving the goals laid out in the plan and were required to provide a written reflection on their progress toward achieving these goals at the end of the year. Furthermore, a majority of teachers were also automatically subjected to a more rigorous and formal assessment process every three years, rather than the suggested five to seven. In short, the report suggested an evaluation process that was less robust than the one that was already in place.

Finally, the report called for the responsibility for teacher discipline and teaching standards to be taken from the NSTU and given to the Department of Education. But that responsibility *already* rested firmly in the hands of the department. When it comes to the practice of teaching, the NSTU does not have the authority to create accountability measures, nor does it have the authority to hold underperforming teachers accountable. The rationale for this is simple — teachers do not work for the NSTU, but are employed by the various regional educational authorities. The employer has the right, and, indeed, the duty, to create a process by which teachers are evaluated. The role of the union is to ensure that the process is followed.

The fact that this paper contained such fundamental errors should have been cause to question everything that it contained. However, with a maddening predictability, little weight was given to the misinformation, and the recommendations — although based upon significant errors — became the focus of media coverage, political debate and public conversation. The recommendations included setting up a College of Teachers, creation of a branch of the Department of Education to oversee teacher education programs and, perhaps not surprisingly considering the source, the removal of principals and other supervisory personnel from the NSTU.

Even when the minister herself publicly pointed out the paper's errors, she stopped short of criticizing the entire document.[20] She suggested that her government would "consider" the recommendations and agreed that having principals and teachers in the same union "presented some challenges" despite the absence of any objective evidence that this was in fact the case. Thus, the neoliberal view of how the education system should be structured was given tremendous credence, even when presented through a flawed and error-ridden report.

PISA 2012

One of the hallmarks of GERM is its focus on large-scale, standardized assessment. As previously discussed, one of the most widely known of these is managed by the Organisation for Economic Co-operation and Development (OECD). It has developed a system for evaluating students' ability in three key subject areas — reading, math and science — through the Programme for International Student Assessment or, as it is more commonly known, PISA.

Countries sign up to become members of the OECD, and the organization looks after the creation, distribution and marking of the tests, which are administered to fifteen-year-old students across the globe every three years. Countries are ranked by how well their students score on a comparative scale and the results are distributed across member countries. Canada has its own version of a standardized test, which is also distributed every three years and is similarly focused on core subjects. Our assessment is called the Pan-Canadian Assessment Programme, or PCAP, and it is coordinated by the Council of Ministers of Education, Canada (CMEC).

The PISA tests have taken place for about two decades and the focus varies each time. In 2012, the spotlight was on math, and when the results were released in December 2013 they showed that Canada as a whole had slipped in the rankings, falling out of the top ten to thirteenth place internationally. This set off national alarm bells and saw provinces from east to west scrambling to identify the problem.[21] In predictable fashion, business leaders were among the most vocal critics. Former federal politician and multi-millionaire John Manley called the development a national crisis.[22] To get a sense of the potential impact of Manley's words, at the time he was the CEO of the Canadian Council of Chief Executives (now the Business Council of Canada).[23] That organization's ranks are populated only by Canada's wealthiest individuals running the country's corporations who together control about $4.5 trillion in assets.

Nova Scotia had fallen in the rankings comparative to other provinces as well, finishing in sixth place nationally with an average score of 497. However, in her initial press release, the minister of education sounded few alarm bells. Although she did say that the math scores were a "concern," she also stated, "Our students have again demonstrated that on the world stage, we are among the best."[24] This summation stands out in stark contrast to later comments made by the minister around the failing public education system.

The press outlets were almost universal in their condemnation, characterizing Canada's results in math as "the lowest scores yet." Many commentators were quick to arrive at these conclusions and several comparisons were made between the 2012 results (Canadian students achieved a mean score of 518 — 24 points above the OECD average) and our scores of 512 in 2009, 506 in 2006 and 515 in 2003. What was lost on the casual observer was that in both 2009 and 2006, math was tested as a "minor" domain. As such, questions that looked at math proficiency are almost like an "add on" to the main tests, which measured science proficiency in 2006 and reading in 2009. Tests like PISA often contain warnings that caution against drawing conclusions around the results of minor domains, but understanding the relative value of data requires at least some level of familiarity with large-scale assessment. Unfortunately, we live in a "sound-bite" world, and the resounding message was that our schools were failing in math.

As is often the case, the results did contain some good news for our education system, but most of that was lost in the conversation around where we placed. For example, the OECD tabulates its data in numerous ways, including looking at the range in scores from low achievers to high achievers. The smaller the range between these two extremes, the more equitable the education system. At the time, little was made of the fact that Nova Scotia had the most equitable education system in the country.[25,26]

2013 Test Scores

This next round of large-scale standardized assessment results played a far greater role in GERM establishing a firm foothold in our province and the onset of Unsupported Deficiency Syndrome. In October 2014, the results of the Pan-Canadian Assessment Program (PCAP) tests were released.[27] The PCAP test is delivered nationally every three years and tests students' abilities in reading, science and math. In 2013, the major domain was science, and the test looked at three areas (known as competencies) in particular: science inquiry, problem solving and scientific reasoning. The test was further broken down into four subcategories: nature of science, life science, physical science and Earth science. There were sections of the test that measured English and math, but they were, once again, considered "minor domains" and were accompanied by a warning that encouraged caution when examining data from these areas of the test.

As with PISA, the data revealed Nova Scotia had done respectably well. The PCAP had set the Canadian average at a score of 500, and Nova Scotia scored 492. Not surprisingly considering the correlation between strong socio-economic standing and positive test scores, Alberta and Ontario had outpaced Nova Scotia by a healthy margin. However, the race for bronze had been close. BC had come in third, but was only eight percentage points higher than Newfoundland and Labrador and nine higher than Nova Scotia. In a tight race, Nova Scotia had ranked fifth.

Looking more closely at the results, there was more good news as far as the national rankings were concerned. In the subcategory of physical science, Nova Scotia was virtually tied for third place with BC — again, good news considering our relative economic standing. In Earth science, Nova Scotia beat out BC (again behind Ontario and Alberta), but came in behind PEI and Newfoundland. When it came to nature of science, Nova Scotia was in a virtual tie for fourth place, behind the big three, but was edged out again by Newfoundland. In the final category, life science, we were placed sixth, losing fifth spot to Saskatchewan.

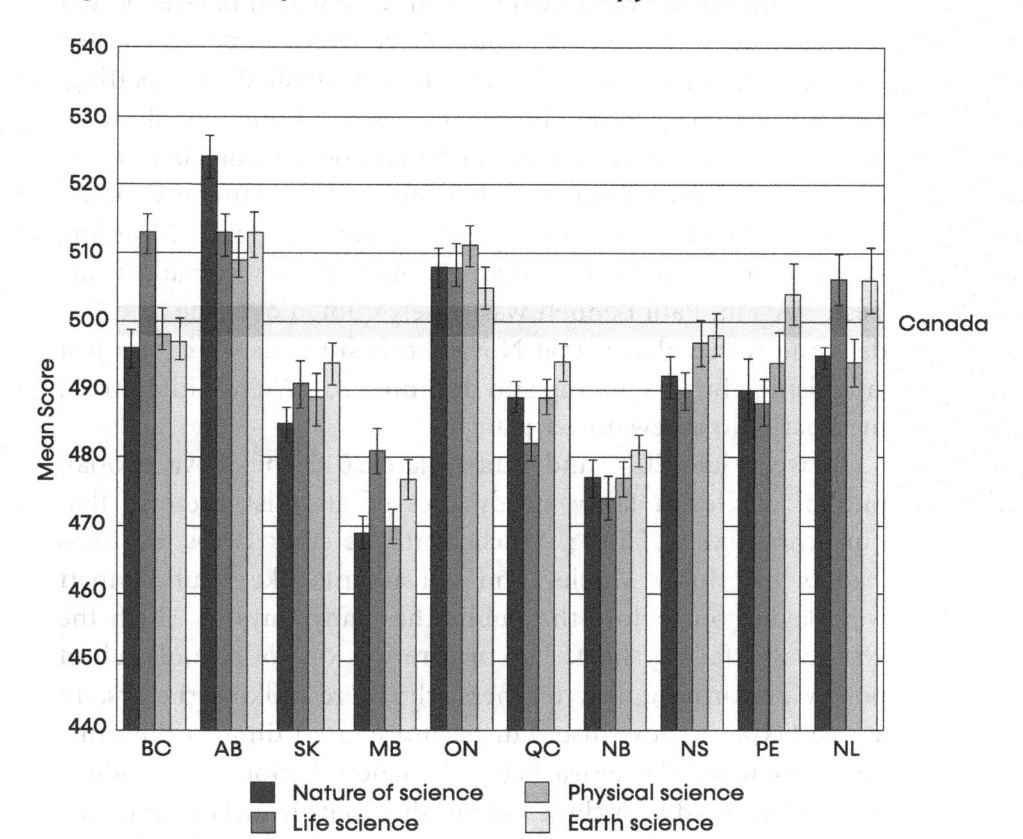

Figure 1: Results by sub-domain in science by jurisdiction

[Bar chart showing mean scores by sub-domain (Nature of science, Life science, Physical science, Earth science) for jurisdictions BC, AB, SK, MB, ON, QC, NB, NS, PE, NL, with Canada reference line around 500.]

Source: CMEC/Kathryn O'Grady and Koffi Houme (2014), *PCAP 2013: Report on the Pan-Canadian Assessment of Science, Reading, and Mathematics*, page 24.

When it came to overall performance in the subcategories, PCAP set a score of 500 as the expectation for Canada, and Nova Scotia had scored 497 in physical science and 498 in Earth science. Nature of science and life science were 490 and 492 respectively.

The PCAP is scored on a four-point scale, and to meet national standards students should attain a level two or above. Ninety-one per cent of Nova Scotia students reached that benchmark. By comparison, Alberta saw 93 per cent of students do the same thing, Ontario 94 per cent, and BC also 91 per cent.

In short, Nova Scotia held its own. One would have expected that such an achievement would have been, if not cause for celebration, at least cause for a bit of self-satisfied back patting. Not so. Headlines across the province decried the poor showing in math and had little, if anything to say about results in science. Media headlines included such gems as "NS Students Doing Better in Math but Not Up to National Average"[28] and "Middling Results for Nova Scotia Grade 8 Students on Canada-Wide Test."[29] Again, Paul Bennett was widely quoted over the next few days and raised alarms that Nova Scotia students were "not just languishing but stagnating and declining . . . We're sliding from mediocrity to a new, lower plateau."[30]

Between late 2012 and mid-to-late 2015 the Nova Scotian public was fed a fairly steady diet of alarmist rhetoric that our schools were failing. Much as in the early 1990s, business leaders like John Manley and consultants like Paul Bennett were laying out before the public the many ways in which the system was falling short. The picture was one of schools full of poorly performing, lazy teachers who were milking the system at the taxpayers' expense. Furthermore, according to the same commentators, the Nova Scotia Teachers Union had made it impossible to address these failings due to its ironclad contract.

This barrage of negativity is a hallmark of the neoliberal think tanks, and it has a proven track record of success. Remember the neoliberal fundamental belief that if a market does not exist, it should be created. If the public believes the current system is doing well, there will be little appetite to tear it down. Thus, the neoliberal think tanks take a slow and methodical approach, creating fear about poor student achievement, uncertainty about the quality of teachers and doubt that anyone is doing anything to address the issues. They had been saying for many years that our schools were failing, and the public was starting to believe them. Once that began to happen, the neoliberals could frame their market-based education policies as the solution, claiming all the while that they, not the people working within the system, had the kids' best interest at heart.

It was during this period, a time when the neoliberal campaign was at its peak, that the government embarked upon a full-fledged review of the public education system. The primary method of gathering information was a public opinion survey, which asked Nova Scotians what they thought about their public schools and the people who staffed them. Through this survey the effectiveness of the neoliberal campaign was soon on prominent display.

CHAPTER 7
The Political Response: The Minister's *Action Plan* (2014–2015)

As the second decade of the new millennium dawned, teachers across North America found themselves embroiled in often bitter labour disputes, facing governments who seemed less and less willing to honour previous commitments and a public that seemed less and less willing to support them.

Across the country, many Canadian teachers were facing governments looking for a convenient scapegoat to blame for years of poor decision making. In part because of constant pressure by those who supported a free-market system, public education had become a favourite target of politicians. One of the most glaring examples of austerity-on-the-backs-of-teachers-trend was in Ontario in 2012, where teachers were forced to accept an agreement that involved wage freezes and a reduction of sick time.[1]

In Nova Scotia there were similar developments. In 2009 the provincial NDP government, often framed as a friend of labour, embarked on a series of austerity measures. Using the catchphrase "putting kids and learning first," the province saw about $65 million, according to some reports, removed from the education budget.[2] During a debate on the proposed cuts, which were being harshly criticized by the teachers' union, the NDP education minister claimed in the provincial legislature that it was her government, not the union, that was most concerned about children.[3] That a traditionally labour-friendly government would frame a union as "the bad guys" gives some sense of the extent to which neoliberalism had spread across party lines.

By the 2013 provincial election, the hope that had accompanied the NDP's arrival into office had faded. With the death of federal NDP leader Jack Layton in 2011, the party had lost a great deal of the charisma that had seen it win a historic provincial majority in 2009, the first for the NDP in the province. Austerity budgets from NDP Finance Minister Graham Steele had been poorly received, and even though there were some wins during their time in office, particularly the awarding of a major federal government shipbuilding contract to the Halifax Shipyard, the party was losing ground.

In its place, there was a resurgence of the Liberals under leader Stephen McNeil. McNeil had been relatively unknown up until his selection as party leader, and his easy style and rustic roots played well to the public. The Liberals swept into power in 2013, winning a solid majority government.[4]

When McNeil announced his cabinet, there was a general sense of approval for the premier's choice of minister of education. Karen Casey was a long-time politician, a former educator and administrator and had served as minister of education with the Progressive Conservative Party prior to crossing the floor to join the Liberals in 2011. With the new government promising to honour collective bargaining and a new minister with a relevant background, teachers began to feel that there was perhaps, finally, some relief in sight. It would not be long before that hope was decisively shattered.

On February 18, 2014, the government announced that it would be embarking upon the first full review of the education system in the province in twenty-five years and would be creating a panel for that purpose.[5] The announcement of the panel, initially met with cautious optimism, turned quickly to concern about the qualifications of the individuals charged with this responsibility. The panel was made up of five people who, at the most generous, had only an arms-length knowledge of the daily realities of the school system. There was one retired teacher, a Mi'kmaw mother of three, a vice-president of finance from a local university, a former business vice-president and a consultant based in Toronto. Critics of the panel pointed out several concerns with the experience of the panel members, not the least of which was the absence of anyone who was actively teaching. As well, there seemed to be no serious consideration of minority groups, which should figure prominently in such a discussion. Although the group did include a Mi'kmaw mother, there was no real sense that she had been chosen by anyone from the Mi'kmaw community to be their representative. There was also concern that there was no representation from the teachers' union or the Nova Scotia School Board Association.

Concerns were also raised about the close associations of Toronto-based consultant Kyle Hill with several pro-privatization organizations. The firm he worked for, Boston Consulting Group, had been heavily pushing the privatization agenda in the US. One of the firm's pet projects was an organization called "Teach for America," a non-profit that specializes in placing new university graduates in hard-to-staff schools in the US. With practices reminiscent of the Peace Corps, these graduates, who do not need a bachelor of education qualification, serve in communities for two years, after which they are free to find alternative careers, content that they have done their part for the betterment of society. Teach for America has been widely criticized for a variety of reasons, not the least of which includes inflicting some fairly heavy damage on the US public education system.[6] The organization has been accused of displacing licenced teachers in areas like Chicago and New Orleans, and of being a tool used by reformists to dismantle public education. The discovery that Kyle Hill had been one of the founders of a new not-for-profit called "Teach for Canada,"[7] closely modelled on its American cousin, did little to calm the province's educational waters.[8]

The committee began its work by launching a series of public consultations on the state of public education in the province. One of the linchpins of the endeavour was an online opinion survey that sought public input, with a heavy emphasis on the word "opinion." It was available on the government's website and open to all Nova Scotians to complete. This was a matter of grave concern for those of us in the field who worried that major decisions would be made based on what the general public thought they knew about the system at a time when Unsupported Deficiency Syndrome was heavily at play.

The majority of Canadians have, on average, twelve years of experience in public education upon which to draw in order to judge its merits. The challenge is not *that* people form an opinion of schools based on their experiences, but *when* and *how* they do so. As far as the when is concerned, relying on judgments made about experiences during an individual's most formative and turbulent years is not likely to yield the most objective results. When it comes to the how of the matter, I refer again to Unsupported Deficiency Syndrome and the questionable wisdom of basing decisions about public education on public opinion alone. The media at the time were rife with weakly supported claims of how schools were failing, and the impact on public opinion was soon on prominent display.

The survey opened benignly enough, with a simple self-identification piece, followed by a request for information from respondents on their overall satisfaction with Nova Scotia's public education system. The choices ranged from "Very Satisfied" to "Very Dissatisfied," and there was a spot on the survey for written comments. In the next section the survey began to explore controversial waters. This section asked respondents to express their opinions on "Teaching and Learning" in the province, and was, tellingly, the largest section of the survey. The first three statements requested opinions on whether "Students receive highly effective teaching," if "Students are engaged in their learning" and if "Students receive helpful feedback" about their schoolwork.

The next section of the survey asked questions about teacher qualifications, which again seemed driven by the talk of the time rather than any verifiable concern. One question asked respondents their opinion on how well teachers were "Prepared to respond to the needs of their students" and specified that the survey was looking for the public to weigh in on the extent to which teachers had the right skills for their grade level or subject area.

Had the Department of Education wanted to accurately determine how well teachers' skills matched with their assignment, they had the power to do so. Finding out what the public *thought* about teacher expertise as opposed to actually checking smacked much more of looking for a predictable result rather than carrying out a legitimate review of the education system.

The next section of the survey was also somewhat concerning for those of us in the field, not for what it asked but for what it didn't. The section began by asking respondents for an overall judgment of how effective Nova Scotia curriculum was in ensuring that "students are learning the right skills" and was followed by three points dedicated to, in order, math skills, literacy skills and problem-solving skills. Any other objective for curriculum, such as creating responsible citizens or teaching kids to express themselves through the arts, was apparently not worthy of comment. As well, four of the questions in this section were dedicated to asking how well schools were preparing students to enter the workforce. That so much of this once-in-twenty-five-years review of the public-education system focused on the system's ability to produce workers, as opposed to, say, critical thinkers, strongly suggested the influence of GERM and neoliberalism.

Approximately 19,000 Nova Scotians responded to the survey. The data was then supplied to the panel. In October 2014, the results of the survey were released in a report to the minister, titled *Disrupting the Status Quo: Nova Scotians Demand a Better Future for Every Student.*[9]

The report was heavily inclined to the neoliberal reform mantra. As a justification of its call for major changes, the panel made a specific reference to both large-scale assessment results and the need for the system to allow students to become more competitive. The panel wrote, "[These] recommendations constitute a significant change for the management of our school system. There is no other choice. The assessment results of Nova Scotian students reveal that our students are not performing well in comparison to other provinces. Given that our youth need to succeed in a competitive world, this is deeply disturbing."[10] The introduction to the report went on to state, "Staying the course will result in Nova Scotia continuing to slip relative to others, leaving our students at a competitive disadvantage in Canada and in the world. Quite simply, far too many students are without the skills in mathematics and literacy they will need to prosper in education and the labour market."[11] The entire report was couched in the language of Fear, Uncertainty and Doubt. The authors of the report relied heavily on the results from the 2013 PCAP science test, ignoring both the positive side of the results and the warnings about the dangers of drawing conclusions about the use of minor domains. They framed the scores as being wholly substandard and recommended a total of thirty changes that they felt would improve public education. These were divided up into seven broad themes that included a call to strengthen the curriculum to "transform teaching and learning" and a call for an increased focus on making "high quality teaching the norm in every classroom."

The rub for teachers was two-fold. They had gone into this exercise with the expectation that some substantive change would take place that would improve their lot, but instead the report spoke of a deficit in teaching. The recommendations were based on public opinion and not empirical evidence or objective research. For example, under the curriculum heading, there were calls for "the early elementary curriculum to focus primarily on foundational skills in mathematics and literacy,"[12] which was already a major focus of that level. There was also a suggestion that the junior-high curriculum be revised "to ensure that options are available that are engaging and relevant in order to better meet the developmental needs and interests of students,"[13] with, again, no empirical consideration of the extent to which the current curriculum was either engaging or relevant.

Of greater concern were the recommendations around teaching. Much like the test score reporting, the idea that our schools were filled with underachieving teachers had been a topic of media attention during this time period, with much of the conversation being driven by AIMS. Indeed, one of the quotes in the report is telling of the pitfalls of allowing public opinion to drive educational policy, particularly during a time when media sensationalism was setting the tone for the discourse. In part, the quote read: "Ineffective/disengaged teachers need to go. There appears to be no accountability in managing a teacher's performance . . . other than acceptance, which is totally unacceptable."[14]

This quote was attributed to a parent, cherry-picked out of presumably hundreds of comments with no way to validate its authenticity. Assuming that it was submitted by a concerned parent, one wonders how this conclusion was formed. Was this a case of a parent who had a bad experience with their own teacher as a child, or a bad experience with their child's teacher? Outside of these possibilities, there would be little way for a parent to know about the existing practices around holding teachers accountable other than what had been reported in the media.

The panel expanded on this concern and made recommendations about improving the entrance requirements for bachelor of education degrees, which implied that the current entrance requirements were not stringent enough. The authors claimed that bachelor of education programs themselves were not preparing new teachers for "the realities of today's classrooms and the range of student needs" without providing any evidence for that conclusion.[15]

The extent to which speculation and misinformation was driving the report was further evidenced when, later in the document, it was recommended that the province "Implement a provincial performance management system that recognizes teaching excellence, supports professional growth, and empowers school boards to dismiss teachers when performance issues warrant," which strongly echoed the AIMS position paper of a few months earlier.[16] The fact that boards already had the power to dismiss teachers seemed to be unknown to the panel. As if to finally seal the deal, as it were, on the pervasiveness of the neoliberal ideology, the report proposed the following:

> *At present, personnel in the education sector are managed through a system where many supervisory staff (e.g., principals, supervisors, directors, and superintendents of school boards) are members of the same union as teachers. The effectiveness of any managerial system is ultimately dependent upon the skills of individual managers. The panel observes, however, that the practice of supervisory staff being members of the same bargaining unit as the employees they supervise is unusual by accepted labour relations practices.*
>
> *A more effective approach to managing the system would call for a model where supervisory staff are not active members of the same union as teachers. This, in turn, would provide a more structured approach to issues of hiring, work assignments, professional development, and performance management.*[17]

This recommendation came with no evidence to support the declaration that this "approach to managing" would be more effective. There was no data to suggest that the current "approach to issues of hiring, work assignments, professional development and performance management" was not well structured and effective. Finally, and probably most egregiously, the survey had not included a single question about the model of management that was in place at the time. Of the three questions that directly asked people to weigh in on classroom teachers, none mentioned the supervisory process.

Recommendations in this area reportedly relied on comments from the respondents, which had undoubtedly been heavily influenced by the conversations that were happening in the media. There are few other avenues available for the public to form any opinion of such inside workings, so in the absence of direct experience in the system, they had come to accept the idea that the system was flawed as truth.

This is not a criticism of the public, but rather a reflection of the power of repetitive messaging.

Keeping in mind that this survey was distributed at the same time that the AIMS report on teacher accountability was being extensively covered by the media, it is no wonder that the public was so quick to pass judgement. With a nod to Hayek, it would seem that a secondhand dealer in ideas was indeed influencing the public narrative. Similar to the approach taken in *Fox in the Schoolhouse*, simply stating loudly enough, firmly enough and often enough that a problem existed in the current structure was leading to the change AIMS had so long desired. The days of the NSTU including principals amongst its members were numbered.

There were other recommendations from the panel, of course, and not all were in the neoliberal vein. But in examining the province as a case of neoliberal creep, this is a textbook example of how the ideology is spread. The conclusion was that our teachers were underprepared and poorly managed, and in order to save our schools, things had to change.

The minister of education soon responded. On January 29, 2015, the Department of Education and Early Childhood

Development released *The Three Rs: Renew, Refocus, Rebuild: Nova Scotia's Education Action Plan*.[18] If there was any hope that anything other than neoliberally influenced opinion would be reflected by the government's actions, the minister's comments closed that door. She criticized the system for not having "kept pace" and explained that "Time and again, test results show our students are falling behind in math and literacy, nationally and internationally." She went on to explain how the system has "lost credibility" in the eyes of the public and that what was required was more accountability for tangible results.

The plan was centred around four key areas, or pillars:

- A modern education system

- An innovative curriculum

- Inclusive school environments

- Excellence in teaching and leadership

Although there were a number of initiatives that could produce positive changes in the classroom, there was a clear GERM tone to the document. There was a great deal of discussion around testing and evaluation, as well as renewed commitment to focus on numeracy and literacy skills. Furthermore, tucked into its pages was a series of suggestions that were ominous for teachers. These were contained on what would become known as "Page 17," where the minister had listed a series of "issues that relate to legislation and collective agreements" that would require either agreement from or negotiation with the teachers' union.

Two of the recommendations dealt with teacher professional development (PD) and suggested that the government wanted more control over how PD money was spent. In addition, there was a recommendation that the school year be lengthened so that teachers could pursue PD during the summer months, instead of during the school year.

For years, teachers had been able to apply for funding to take self-directed professional development from a fund that was guaranteed under their union contract. This fund was managed by a committee of an equal number of representatives from the Regional Education Centres and the NSTU. Teachers could apply for whatever program or conference they wish, but applications required approval from the committee before funding was granted.

The fact that teachers enjoyed a fair bit of autonomy around how they pursued professional development had been a sore spot for successive governments, and there had been several attempts to take control of this fund through the collective bargaining process. The NSTU had no issue with teachers having to apply for access to the fund, nor was there any concern expressed that the department and the union had equal say in the approval process. However, as this was a costed, negotiated benefit, the union opposed giving complete control to the department. That this frequent government negotiating "ask" made it into the recommendations for improving education raised questions in union circles about the sincerity and the purpose of the review.

This type of professional development is not the same and should not be confused with the previously discussed licence upgrades that were such a hot topic at the time. Where teachers did enjoy some autonomy over their own professional development choices, their ability to pursue further education for the purpose of upgrading their qualifications was more limited. The power to approve or deny those upgrades rested solely with the Department of Education.

It's easy to imagine why, considering the timing of the survey, the public would comment negatively on teacher professional development, unaware of the difference between professional development and the licence upgrades. Both might be funded, but only one — the upgrade — resulted in a pay raise. The government, however, was not operating under the same inaccurate assumptions. The implication of the report seemed to be that if the government took a larger role in teacher professional development (over which they then exercised only partial control), issues like the Drake University upgrades (over which they then exercised complete control) would no longer occur, or so they would have liked the public to believe. The government's proposed improvement to the system smacked strongly of political posturing and felt like a way for them to remove benefits from teachers without having to bother with collective bargaining.

The recommendation around having PD days in the summer months was also suspect. Parents sometimes resent school closures for PD days, but having the days embedded in the school year was in line with best educational practice. Professional development works best if a teacher learns about a particular educational theory one day and then returns to the classroom the next day to implement it. Being immersed in the day-to-day realities of the job, teachers can align what they are learning with what will work for their students. The suggestion made by the government that this work should happen outside of the school calendar seemed to be more about scoring political points than about improving education.

On teacher accountability, the *Action Plan* was even more ambitious. Not only did the minister suggest that the province should generate a new way of certifying teachers, but also bolstered the public perception that the current system of evaluating teacher performance was flawed. She called for the "creation of a robust system for teacher performance management," a more direct link between teacher credentials and teaching assignments and strengthening the process by which poor teaching performance was addressed. This indication that current systems were inadequate was a hard pill for teachers to swallow.

In order to ensure that these new accountability practices be properly managed, the final section of the report dealt with the creation of a new set of teacher standards that would be developed and implemented as part of what was referred to as a new "performance management system." These standards would be a major part of the teacher evaluation system and would be administered by principals, whom, as if to finally connect the neoliberal dots, the report suggested should be removed from the union.

An initial reaction of shock and disbelief to this plan was quickly replaced by anger. Many teachers had filled out the survey and had placed their faith in the assumption that if they did so, the government would address their growing concerns around such things as class composition and increased data collection. What they got, however, were recommendations that many saw as calling into question their professionalism while providing few concrete suggestions to improve working conditions. Considering that some of the final suggestions, such as those centering around professional development, had not even been part of the survey, the intent of the report became even more suspect. Indeed, since no one outside of the government had actually seen the survey results, that these recommendations were generated from the information gathered was a matter of faith rather than of fact. When the survey data was finally released to the NSTU months later, it was so redacted that it was of little use in testing any government claims of validity.

In 2015, the Liberal government launched its brand new vision of education for Nova Scotia using both language and methodology that mirrored *A Nation at Risk* from thirty years before. Without any substantive evidence, and in the absence of any measure for success other than a selective interpretation of large-scale data and even less reliable opinion surveys, the message was clear: our schools were failing, and something had to be done.

The *Action Plan* laid out an ambitious attack on the teachers' contract and ways to increase teacher accountability, emphasize math and literacy skills and increase the stature of standardized testing in the province. The minister's *Action Plan* aligned almost exactly with the neoliberal framework of educational reform.

If these initiatives had been happening in isolation, perhaps the situation would not have appeared so dire. However, while teachers faced the advance of the neoliberal GERM on this front, another concentrated attack was being waged, and it had the organization in the best position to defend teachers against GERM directly in its crosshairs.

CHAPTER 8
A Clash of Agendas: The Teacher Job Action (2016–2017)

When it comes to implementing neoliberal educational reforms, one of the most common targets for attacks are teachers' unions. Commonly, when reformists start to gain ground, teachers' unions are vilified as being in the fight only to advance their own agenda, as opposed to advancing the cause of public education. This hostility toward organized labour harkens back to Hayek. It is not surprising that when it came to Nova Scotia's public school system, the GERM surge was accompanied by an onslaught against the NSTU, the likes of which the province had never seen.

October 2013 had been a historic month for Nova Scotia. The voters of the province ousted the first-ever incumbent New Democratic Party (NDP) government under Darrell Dexter and replaced it with the Liberal Party and Premier Stephen McNeil.[1] It also marked the beginning of what would soon become a concentrated attack against all organized labour in the province.

Although McNeil had been on record during the election campaign as being in favour of free and fair collective bargaining, not long into the Liberal mandate their neoliberal ideology began to emerge. Mere months after taking office, the McNeil Liberals proved that they were willing to legislate rather than negotiate when dealing with bargaining units.[2] They first passed legislation to end a strike by homecare workers in February 2014; then in March, the Liberals passed the *Essential Health and Community Services Act*, an essential services bill.[3] This ended the threat[4] of a nurses' strike in the Capital District Health Authority and was quickly followed by legislation to reduce the number of bargaining units that would represent health-care workers.[5]

In 2015, Finance Minister Randy Delorey alerted union leaders that the government would achieve a balanced budget for Nova Scotia taxpayers without raising taxes, and by this time it was very apparent that the government was more than willing to legislate in order to achieve their ends. Emboldened by his success against the nurses, McNeil announced that his government would be offering all government worker bargaining units a 2 per cent wage increase over five years, and that if the deal was not accepted, he would legislate rather than go to arbitration. One of McNeil's talking points was that he would not allow any third party to dictate to him what the province could afford. This austerity approach aligned itself with the neoliberal analysis being pushed by AIMS that public-sector spending was out of control in the province.

In this climate a contract offer was made to the Nova Scotia Teachers Union in fall 2015. Even with the previous dealings as a basis on which to predict the path negotiations would take, the offer presented to the bargaining team of the NSTU was less than appealing. Not only was the government looking to establish a lower-than-inflation rate wage pattern, offering the 2 per cent increase over five years, but they were also looking to phase out a long-term service award — a long-standing retirement savings plan. This retirement benefit had been achieved many years prior and was governed by a number of conditions, depending upon the date that teachers had been hired and in which board they worked for. In general, most teachers were entitled to receive upon retirement a payment equal to 1 per cent of their salary per year, up to a maximum of about thirty years.

As another indicator of how the negotiations would go, the government also included in its offer some of the more controversial aspects from the infamous Page 17 of the minister's *Action Plan*. These included lengthening the school year by five days, asserting more power over teacher professional development and removing principals from the NSTU. The inclusion of these asks seemed to validate the view that the neoliberal doctrine advanced by AIMS had, by this time, been completely adopted at the highest levels of government.

The process that brought Nova Scotia to this point was textbook. A right-wing think tank that supported the development of free markets had made recommendations for educational reform over the course of several years. These ideas for "improving" the system, although largely unsubstantiated, had received lots of media attention and had become part of the general conversation. When the public was surveyed on their views, these same, unsubstantiated ideas were reflected back as solutions to problems within the system — problems that had been heavily overstated, if not completely fabricated, by the neoliberal movement. Then, as the *coup de grâce*, these same ideas appeared in contract negotiations and were the basis of government policy.

At this point, some teachers began to fear things were not going to go well in this round of negotiations, but most had faith in the power of the collective bargaining process. Facing what was undoubtedly going to be a tough round of negotiations, the NSTU executive stepped outside its normal playbook and hired labour lawyer Ron Pink to act as their chief negotiator with the Liberal government. The rationale for this move was straightforward. Anticipating that the Liberal government would be taking a no-holds-barred approach to bargaining, the provincial executive of the NSTU, all teacher volunteers, decided they needed professional help. Traditionally, NSTU negotiations were handled by a team made up of staff officers (former teachers who are hired by, trained by and work for the NSTU) and members of the provincial executive, including the president.

After a series of negotiations, the negotiator went back to the union leadership with an offer of a 3 per cent wage raise over four years combined with an end of the service award. All other asks — both from the teachers' side and the government's — would be taken off the table.

Not only were teachers being offered what many saw as a substandard deal, but they were also having any concerns they had wanted addressed by the government disregarded. Teachers had been finding themselves not only under increasing criticism, but also under ever-increasing pressure in their classroom. The series of accountability initiatives as well as the minister's *Action Plan* had left them feeling more than a bit underappreciated and undervalued. To have the government dismiss the idea of having some of these issues rectified through collective bargaining added insult to injury, particularly since only through the collective bargaining process could such concerns be addressed with any sort of certainty.

Furthermore, many of the government's asks would have increased teacher workload. For example, the government wanted teachers to supervise students over the lunch hour, wanted to increase the duties of the teacher as per the *Education Act* and wanted teachers to report to school on storm days. In exchange for abandoning these contentious asks, teachers were being offered a pay raise that was not just below inflation, but was also worth less than they were losing through the removal of the service award.

This deal was recommended to teachers by the NSTU executive, and put forward for a ratification vote. But when the details of the proposed contract were released to the teachers, it was met with a general sense of unrest. I choose that word specifically, because there was still, among many teachers, almost an ambivalence toward contract negotiations. This may sound strange to those outside of the teaching world, particularly in light of recent events, but over time teachers had become somewhat unplugged from the process. For a number of years, contract negotiations had been, if not necessarily collegial, at least somewhat predictable. They usually brought about some small gains here and there, but were, for the most part, fairly benign. Even in years when there were cutbacks to education funding, it was the cutbacks, not the contract that garnered ire. Teachers believed that their contract was safe.

However, this time around, teachers began questioning why the deal, which was essentially concessionary, was recommended by NSTU leadership. It was then revealed that the negotiator had brought the deal to the provincial executive with a warning. The message from the government was simple and effective. Teachers had been told to either take the offer or the government would legislate it into being. In fact, union lore is that the government side had suggested that the legislation already existed in draft form. Considering the long list of offensive items that had been withdrawn, and facing what they had been told was certain legislation, the union executive — again, a body made up entirely of volunteer classroom teachers — reluctantly recommended that the membership accept the offer. A vote was scheduled for December 1.

As the days passed, social media (which played a major role in events as they unfolded) began to buzz about the offer. Once this ball began to roll, it became a veritable freight train within days, pushed along by commentary from some more traditional news sources. On November 24, a letter was published in *The Chronicle Herald*, written by former first vice-president and NSTU presidential candidate Eric Boutilier.[6] In his letter, Boutilier urged the membership to reject the offer, calling it "the worst tentative deal in recent history," and called on the NSTU leadership to "show some backbone." This was quickly followed up in *The Chronicle Herald* by a letter from the lead negotiator to the entire NSTU membership, urging them to accept the offer, pointing out that there was a possibility that if the offer were rejected, the government would legislate a less attractive deal.[7] As the debate heated up, staff rooms across the province hummed with discussion around the contract, and teachers began to engage.

The deciding factor in the eventual outcome of this first vote, however, was an exceptionally unusual, if not unprecedented, move by a group of six past NSTU presidents, led by spokesperson Brian Forbes. The group issued an official statement on November 27 in which they declared the deal to be suspect.[8] They expressed concern that, since there was a groundswell rising against accepting the offer, there was a very real possibility that the contract could be rejected. They urged the NSTU to place the vote on hold and for both sides to return to the bargaining table in order to avoid this possibility.

Forbes had been down this road before. Back in 1994, when the Liberal government under John Savage had attacked collective bargaining rights, Forbes had been vocally critical of union leadership. After the ratification of that collective agreement, also heavily influenced by talk of austerity, Forbes was instrumental in setting up a group that called itself the Teacher Action Council (TAC). The group criticized the leadership of the NSTU for allowing the government to essentially have its way with the teachers' contract. Forbes was later elected NSTU president, a position he held from 2000–04.[9] Despite being retired from teaching, he played a pivotal role in the events of 2015–18.

The vote was not delayed. On December 1, 2015, true to Forbes's prediction, 60 per cent of teachers in Nova Scotia voted to reject the contract, which would come to be referred to as TPA1.[10]

This "no" vote caught a great many people off guard. Having teachers reject an offer after it had been recommended by the provincial executive of the union had not happened since 2005, when the membership was upset about changes to the teachers' pension plan. Prior to the vote, some political pundits had declared that McNeil had already achieved a win over organized labour. One commentator who echoed this sentiment was Graham Steele, who had been the province's finance minister with the NDP. As early as November, Steele had declared in an op-ed piece for CBC that the Liberals had "triumphed in public sector negotiations."[11] (He would later admit that his declaration of a McNeil victory in these early stages was a "spectacular error.")

Teachers did not have to wait long for the response from the government to their militancy. Two weeks later, Bill 148 was given a first reading in the House of Assembly. Known as the *Public Service Sustainability Act*, the bill applied to all public-sector employees and decreed that any contract negotiated in the province would be subject to the government's desired wage pattern. It also declared that the long-term service award would be discontinued for all government bargaining units. Interestingly, the government sent Bill 148 though to a third reading on December 18, but it was not enacted. With the legislation safely tucked in their back pockets, the Liberals went back to the bargaining table with the NSTU in January 2016 after the Christmas break.

Negotiations dragged on through the winter and spring of 2016, but as they continued behind the scenes a new element was thrown into the mix. In early January, Brian Forbes set up a Facebook page, Nova Scotia Teachers Speaking Out (NSTSO). Originally envisioned as a place where teachers could turn for an open and frank discussion on the contract issues, the site soon morphed into a place where teachers sought out information on everything from the bargaining process to operational procedures. This information was usually the purview of local presidents and the provincial executive, with each body disseminating information to the members. With the establishing of NSTSO, the traditional means of communicating with the membership was, in effect, replaced.

Although Forbes referred to the site as being a place to "exchange information and concerns," much of the discussion on the page echoed Forbes's early days in the NSTU. In a repetition of the past, many teachers were critical of union leadership and its approach to the collective bargaining process, and emotions among the page's contributors ran high. Concerns were vast and varied, but seemed focused on a few key themes, most notably questioning why the provincial executive had brought what was considered a "poor deal" to the membership, and why they had allowed such a pivotal role to be played by lawyer Ron Pink, as opposed to having "teachers bargaining for teachers." The site soon became not just a clearing house for ideas, but also a rallying point for unhappy union members. To say that social media suddenly became a major force for demanding change and asserting influence within the NSTU structure would be an epic understatement. Forbes's experience as a past president gave him tremendous credibility, at not inconsiderable cost to the sitting president, Shelley Morse. By NSTU policy, however, a president can only hold the office for four years. In 2016, Morse's term was done, and a new president, Liette Doucet, was elected.

Early in the 2016–17 school year a second draft agreement was reached, and the provincial executive recommended members accept it. The reaction of teachers this time was swift and angry. In many ways, the offer was the same as the original deal, with teachers seeing the same wage package and a phasing out of the service award. To placate the original concerns expressed by teachers around working conditions, the government offered to set up what it called a "Partnership on Working Conditions" — a body that would address all issues related to such things as data collection and assessment practices. Although this partnership may have been desirable in other times, teachers were becoming more militant. They were resentful of the threat of legislation hanging over their heads and felt that they had little reason to trust that a committee would do much to improve their working conditions. They continued to wish to see some substantive commitment from the government in their contract that classroom conditions would improve if they were going to agree to what amounted to a roll-back in wages.

Although the second deal was arguably better than the first one, the rejection of the first had let the genie out of the bottle.

With the formation of the NSTSO Facebook page, teachers suddenly had a means through which to voice their frustrations around their deteriorating working conditions. These issues ranged from class size to composition to lack of preparation time to many other concerns. Traditionally, teachers had been publicly silent on such issues; however, with the rejection of the first deal, they were becoming emboldened. With good reason to feel slighted by the first offer, they quickly determined that the small improvements in the second deal did not address their issues in any significant way.

On October 4, the second deal was rejected, this time by 70 per cent of union members.[12]

The next several weeks would see moves by both sides, including returning to the bargaining table, requests for conciliation and the appointment of a mediation officer, all with little success. The union's negotiating team was aware that a grassroots uprising was brewing but could secure nothing from the government that would satisfy the membership. Tensions mounted, but teachers were bolstered by a litany of support from other bargaining units and from concerned parents, many of whom sensed that this fight was about much more than superficial gains. Finally, on November 25, talks broke off, with the union leadership expressing tremendous frustration that the government would not move from its stance. Just a few days later, with the threat of legislation still hanging in the air, word went out to teachers that the NSTU would be entering into province-wide job action on December 5.[13]

This job action was to be a combination of a work-to-rule campaign and a partial withdrawal of services. Under the "partial withdrawal of services," teachers were not to participate in several activities that were a regular part of their job. These included attending meetings, accepting student teachers and administering any assessments to students that they had not created, including board- and department-issued standardized tests. The work-to-rule directives forbade teachers from providing services to the schools that fell outside of their contract but that had become commonplace responsibilities for teachers. These included organizing extracurricular activities and supervising students over the lunch hour, none of which were included in teacher contracts.

It says something about the profession that, when it came to such things as student supervision, teachers over the years had become accustomed to not following their own contract. The contract states that teachers cannot be made to supervise students prior to twenty minutes before the instructional day begins and can only be asked to do so for twenty minutes after it ends. The contract also states that teachers cannot be made to provide supervision during the time that students are eating lunch. It was indicative of the times that this particular provision proved so problematic for the government. Over the years, school boards had come to ignore this part of the contract, often allowing bus schedules to determine the arrival and departure time for students. It had become widely accepted practice that teachers would provide supervisory services, regardless of contractual language. When the students arrived, they would be supervised, even if that meant some teachers had to be at work well before the contractually agreed upon twenty minutes, or if they had to work over their lunch hour.

The withdrawal of this service by teachers led to one of the most bizarre twists in this tale and perhaps one of the most bizarre moments in the province's educational history. On Saturday, December 3, just a few days before the job action was set to begin, the minister of education, Karen Casey, held a press conference where she claimed that this withdrawal of voluntary supervisory services would endanger children. Since teachers would not be providing supervision, student safety would be in jeopardy. Using this rationale, she announced that all schools in Nova Scotia would be closed to students on Monday, December 5. At the same time, the government would convene to pass Bill 75, imposing a contract on teachers. With that declaration, the minister had effectively locked students out of school.[14]

The resulting outcry was far beyond what those of us who were involved in this fight could have hoped for. The suggestion that teachers would sacrifice student safety in the name of job action was met with derision and scorn, most of which was directed at the minister. The weekend saw a veritable explosion of social media posts, and MLAs were assaulted with phone calls and emails demanding a return to the bargaining table, with support once again pouring in from parent groups and other unionized workers. On Monday morning, however, the schools were indeed closed to students and the legislature was called to sit and review Bill 75, which was to bring an end to the job action. Again, with a nod to the power of social media, cyberspace was inundated with teachers posting pictures of their empty classrooms accompanied by the hashtag #ReadyToTeach.[15] This was one of the most effective moves of the dispute and saw public opinion swing heavily in favour of the teachers.

Only Nova Scotia Liberal MLAs know what took place in their caucus that day. However, the reported absence from the house of both Stephen McNeil and Karen Casey fanned the flames of speculation that this could become a no-confidence vote. To the angry crowd of protestors who gathered outside Province House, it seemed the party was rattled by the sudden backlash of public anger. By mid-morning, the government had called two recesses, but had not moved forward on the bill. By afternoon, the education minister in the House of Assembly declared that passing Bill 75 was no longer necessary, as the NSTU had modified some of the edicts around work-to-rule to ensure student safety. In yet another embarrassment for the government, it was quickly revealed that the union had already adjusted the work-to-rule directives and that the changes had been sent to the minister's office on Friday, December 2, the day before her original Saturday morning announcement. On Tuesday, December 6, schools in the province re-opened with modified job action directives.[16]

The NSTU had the Liberal government on the mat at this point. There were rumblings from the public when it was revealed that many schools would need to cancel their holiday concerts due to lack of voluntary supervision and that several large-scale school trips were in jeopardy due to the lack of teacher involvement. However, with only a few short weeks left before the Christmas holiday, public support for the teachers' cause seemed relatively solid. Parents, students and members of many other bargaining units had stood, shoulder to shoulder with teachers, marching in the streets to apply pressure. Undoubtedly hoping that the government would offer up some concessions to avoid further turmoil, the NSTU returned to the table, this time with the help of a conciliator. It was not long, however, before the media once again showed its power to influence public opinion.

Shortly after schools returned from the Christmas break, CBC reporter Jean Laroche broke a story about how despite being engaged in their work-to-rule campaign, the NSTU had allowed teachers to continue to attend professional development conferences.[17] That the work-to-rule edicts had included withdrawal of extracurricular services from students was a bone of contention for some parents, particularly when it came to school trips. As it happened, a number of schools had been working toward taking groups of students to France in 2017 to commemorate the anniversary of the battle of Vimy Ridge. One of the directives of the work-to-rule campaign was that teachers not be involved in planning such endeavours (the planning would now need to fall to parents). When it was revealed that the union had allowed a group of teachers to attend a professional development conference in Hawaii over the Christmas holiday, there was a major backlash. It seemed completely unfair that teachers were flying off to exotic destinations like Hawaii, while refusing to organize trips for students.

There was, of course, another side to this story. The application for the conference in Hawaii had been approved by the department, as well as the union, long before the work-to-rule campaign began.

Furthermore, although the location was exotic, the amount of money available to teachers to attend these conferences was fixed — the standard conference grant for teachers in the Halifax region at the time was about $1,300 — so the cost to the taxpayer is the same no matter where the conference.

The most obvious missing element in this story was that the purpose of the job action was to put as much pressure as possible on the government to come to a compromise and to abandon the threatened legislation. Stopping teachers from attending conferences would not advance that cause. As a negotiating tactic, telling teachers to not pursue professional development would have been about as effective as telling them to not take sick days.

All this was, however, lost on the media and the public. The CBC framed the story as teachers taking paid vacations while refusing to plan educational trips for students. The minister was quick to take advantage of the situation, stating in the CBC report: "I don't know how the union can defend that. How can you defend supporting and promoting and protecting activities for teachers and not for students?"[18] This characterization of professional development as "activities" on a par with student field trips served to support an anti-teacher narrative.

Overnight, public opinion, which had been so solidly behind the teachers after the student lockout, was dealt a serious blow. Teachers were framed as milking an already taxed system, and putting their needs ahead of the students'. Although still enjoying the support of many, this story created a cloud of suspicion as to the motives of the teachers' job action and played a huge role in the events that unfolded.

By the end of January, a third tentative agreement was reached and recommended by the provincial executive to union membership, and much like the previous two offers, the reaction was swift and scathing. The salary pattern and the removal of the service award were, again, almost exactly as had been offered previously. What had changed was that now the government was offering something that had not been brought forward in the other contracts. On the table were two extra days of leave for teachers, which, if one did the math, worked out to approximately a 1 per cent increase in available time off per year. These days could have been seen as a fair trade for the loss of the 1 per cent service award but it is indicative of the climate at the time that this part of the offer was met with outrage from some teachers.[19]

Throughout the process, teachers had been trying to get across the message that the conflict was about more than just money. The outcry was not so much about what had been offered, but the way it had been offered and, this time more importantly, what had been left out — specifically language around working conditions. Teachers wanted to see substantive, concrete language that would ensure that they could focus on the job of teaching children. They did not want more time off; they wanted to be able to help their students in their own classrooms, and they wanted a commitment in the new contract. Their experience was that student needs had grown. The number of severe behaviour problems teachers had to deal with seemed to be on the rise, as were incidents of violence. (This trend was later confirmed by the Canadian Teachers' Federation when it was reported, in a 2018 study,[20] that approximately 70 per cent of teachers reported both rates and severity of violence in schools was increasing.) Yet there had been no increase in resources or training to help them cope. Instead, they had seen more time taken up by data collection and standardization, and less time dedicated to helping them help their students. Still stinging from the threat of legislation, this deal provided few concrete improvements to classroom conditions. That did not sit well with teachers.

Finally, there was tremendous concern among teachers about public perception. Having consistently made the argument that their fight for better working conditions was actually about the children's learning conditions, teachers were keenly aware that accepting the two days off work instead of demanding action to benefit students would be seen as self-serving, particularly in light of the Hawaii story. Teachers were reluctant to further undermine public opinion of the profession.

As a final fly in the ointment, there was confusion over what the government was offering. Representatives of the NSTU explained to teachers that these two days could be used as personal days and could effectively be applied to any type of leave not currently covered by the contract. However, during a media scrum in late January, Premier Stephen McNeil contradicted that view and insisted that those days were only meant to be used for marking and preparation for classes.[21] The confusion, the mistrust that had built up between teachers and the government, the fear of weakening public perception and an erosion of faith in the process (constituted by the presentation of what many saw as two substandard offers) led to this deal being voted down by 78 per cent of the membership, the highest rejection to date.

Even at this point, many teachers believed that they would be able to return to the table and continue negotiations. The government took a very different view. After the vote results were released, the premier immediately called the House of Assembly into session. Although initially delayed by a major snow storm, the government once again brought forward Bill 75, slightly modified from its original form. The ensuing week saw the opposition parties attempt to delay the bill, and many teachers, parents and concerned citizens appeared before the Law Amendments Committee to attempt to sway the government from its path. It was all for naught.

On February 21, after what was possibly the largest single demonstration in the province's history and a one-day walk-out by teachers, Bill 75 was passed. In the end, the Liberals did exactly what they had threatened. They had drafted legislation to influence the negotiations with a bargaining unit, and when it became obvious that the members of that group would not give in, they passed that draft legislation into law.[22]

For many teachers, it was a very dark day. They had fought hard, had been vocal in their concerns and had lost. What made the moment more poignant was that so many of them had voted for the Liberal Party in the previous provincial election. Having experienced cutbacks during the Dexter days, many had seen a Liberal government as a viable alternative, particularly considering the premier's comments around collective bargaining. The premier legislating a contract on them was seen by many as a fundamental betrayal of trust.

This sense of betrayal carried teachers forward a few months later when the premier took a very bold political gamble. In late April, McNeil dropped the writ for an election to take place in late May.[23] This caught many off guard, but it was the opportunity teachers had been waiting for. They quickly began to take to social media and call attention to the labour strife of the past two years, placing the blame squarely on McNeil's shoulders and throwing their support behind the other political parties. Another social media group, this one called "Broken Glass Voters," popped up and became another rallying point for those opposed to the current government. The idea that members would rather crawl over broken glass than vote for this particular Liberal government seemed to gather steam as election day approached. Parent groups, concerned citizens and opposition parties all rallied to the cause, once again throwing their support behind the teachers.

For his part, McNeil made no apologies for the decisions he had made during his mandate regarding government contracts with their workers. Displaying little love for organized labour by this point, McNeil doubled down on his bet that he could still count on vilification of the unions to win the day. One of his talking points was that he was elected to represent all Nova Scotians, not just those who happened to belong to a union. This line of reasoning did little to placate teachers, some of whom put themselves forward as candidates to run in their home ridings. As election day approached, the rhetoric around removing the Liberals from office reached a pitch that had not been seen in a long time. Then, on that fateful election day of May 30, 2017, something unexpected happened.

Hardly anyone showed up to vote.

Despite the political furor, less than 54 per cent of eligible voters turned up to cast a ballot — a record low for the province.[24] Although there had been signs early on that McNeil might lose his majority, Nova Scotia's teachers woke up on May 31 to the stark reality that despite all the protests, the impassioned pleas and the political activism, the government had maintained their hold on the house. McNeil had won the election. Although the Liberals had lost seven seats, they managed to retain enough to remain a majority government.

As the 2016–17 school year came to a close, with the McNeil Liberals firmly ensconced in Province House, teachers began to return to what was commonly referred to as "the New Normal." For many, the job action had shown them that they had not been doing a good job of striking a healthy work-life balance. As the labour dispute disappeared in the rear-view mirror, some teachers found themselves taking a step back from all the extras that had traditionally been their lot. There were many anecdotal reports of teachers not taking on the same level of volunteerism that had existed in many schools. In some ways, this was the true cost of the government's insistence on winning the fight. Many things that teachers had been more than willing to do, both for the students and the Department of Education, were suddenly less enticing and teachers became much more selective about how they spent their time.

It was not long, however, before teachers became even more keenly aware of how the premier felt about their stand against his government. In the mayhem of the labour dispute, it was easy to forget the neoliberal agenda of high-stakes testing and higher accountability practices for teachers. But once the dust settled on the 2017 election, these ideas resurfaced with a vengeance.

CHAPTER 9
The Glaze Report: Control and Power to the Province (2017–2019)

As the school year opened in fall 2017, a pall hung over the hallways of many schools. After the militancy and engagement that had been shown during the work-to-rule campaign and the election, teachers reported feeling "different" about their jobs. For many, this had been the first time in their careers that they had engaged in any protest or demonstration. To have fought so hard for change and for recognition and respect, only to have the government enact legislation and win a second majority government, was difficult for many.

In September, things started to settle into "the New Normal." Although the battle had been lost, teachers returned to their classrooms and got back to the business of teaching children. Many of the wounds that had been suffered were still fresh and there were a few challenges to be faced, particularly around the use of teachers' time. After-school meetings, involvement in school activities and, perhaps most challenging, supervision of students all had to be navigated with an eye to the revelations of the work-to-rule campaign. For the most part, although there was still a great deal of resentment toward the government, things began to right themselves in the province's schools. However, it was not long before the government once again used its majority status to impose its will on its teachers.

The new school year began with a new minister of education at the helm. With a fresh majority government in place, Stephen McNeil appointed thirty-four-year-old Zach Churchill to the education position. Churchill had entered politics in 2010, winning his Yarmouth seat in a by-election. Barely twenty-six, Churchill had a somewhat limited political resume, with the only real credit to his name being that he had served as the national director of the Canadian Alliance of Student Associations in 2007 to 2009.[1] Regardless of his political pedigree, Churchill had won the by-election against some stiff competition and held his seat in both the 2013 and 2017 elections.

Churchill lost no time in announcing that there was going to be yet another review of the public education system.[2] This time the focus was to be on school governance, one of the issues raised in the 2015 *Action Plan.* was to examine practices and policies in four key areas that included: administrative structures across the whole system; the efficient use of resources; accountability, transparency and efficiency in decision making; and interagency service delivery. In early October 2017, it was announced that an educational consultant from Ontario, Dr. Avis Glaze, would conduct the review.[3,4]

Glaze, previously employed in Ontario as the education commissioner and a senior advisor to that province's Liberal education leader, seemed an odd choice given that Nova Scotia has no shortage of local educational expertise. Glaze had experience in reviewing other education systems, most notably serving on a panel of experts who were charged with reviewing the education system in Scotland. She had also worked as a superintendent in Ontario, had been appointed as that province's first chief student achievement officer, and had won international awards for her work in the field. However, critics were quick to pick up on Glaze's connections with the Ontario Liberal Party, and her edu-entrepreneurial leanings as founder of a company called Edu-quest International, Inc. Glaze had also been one of the few experts quoted in the original minister's *Action Plan*, suggesting a pre-existing connection between Glaze and the governing Liberals before her appointment was announced.

From the outset, Glaze claimed impartiality. She was adamant that she had been given no coaching by the Liberal government and insisted that she was coming to the province with no preconceived notions of how things could be changed. In one CBC interview, Glaze said, "I don't have an idea of what I'm going to write . . . I want to spend most of my time listening to people first before even thinking of making recommendations."[5] The overall goal was clear: this review was about establishing a system of governance that would "ensure student success."

The task was no small one. Glaze was hired in October and was expected to have a report prepared for the government by December 31. The last time a full review had been done of the education system, it had taken three years. Glaze set out across the province to meet with educational stakeholders. This process lasted less than four weeks, and, according to the final report, included a total of ninety-one meetings with various groups and individuals, including school-board superintendents, educational leaders and local experts in the field, including student mental-health expert Dr. Stan Kutcher; Dr. Jeff Orr, dean of the Faculty of Education at St. Francis Xavier University; and, to the chagrin of many teachers, Dr. Paul W. Bennett. Several town halls were held across the province, and the government conducted another public opinion survey. Finally, there was an effort on Glaze's part to meet with elected school board members and representatives from the Nova Scotia School Board Association.

That final point is of particular importance, as this organization was supportive of the process from the outset. The president of the Nova Scotia School Board Association, Hank Middleton, commented that he was pleased with both Glaze and the review in general. Minister Churchill himself assured Middleton that the government felt the time allotted to the endeavour was adequate and made a point of assuring him that more time would be granted if it became necessary.[6] This seemingly close working relationship between Glaze, the government and the elected school boards during the process gave little indication of what was coming.

Glaze completed her report on schedule, and it was released to the public on January 23, 2018, via press conference. The report was a bombshell.

From the start, the influence of the neoliberal mindset and the educational reformists was evident. Both the document and the press conference were littered with deficit rhetoric and took an alarmist, reactionary tone. The document itself was titled *Raise the Bar: A Coherent and Responsive Education Administrative System for Nova Scotia*, implying that the system which was in place was neither coherent nor responsive.[7] In the introductory paragraphs, in a letter to the minister, Glaze assessed, "There is no time to waste if we are serious about improving Nova Scotia's education system and transforming the province's students into the national and global leaders they must become." Again, this urgency reinforced the view that the current system was failing its students and stressed the idea of global competitiveness. The final line read, "We may not agree on all of the points, yet we all agree on this: the children of Nova Scotia cannot wait," which critics were quick to point out reflected the title of one of Glaze's books, *The Children Cannot Wait*, published a few years prior. The language also called to mind the summary statement from *Horizons*: "We cannot serve the needs of future generations by standing still," published almost twenty-five years previous.

Glaze began her report by repeating the now-familiar mantra that change was necessary because of the poor performance of Nova Scotia students in large-scale national and international assessments. She wrote:

> *While student performance may not immediately be linked to administration and governance, I strongly believe it is. If the system is in a state of conflict or dysfunction, that can only have a negative effect on students . . . when the department and boards are at odds, that can have a corrosive impact. All of that has been happening in Nova Scotia . . . Consider two recent assessments . . . the Pan-Canadian Assessment Program (PCAP), and the Programme for International Student Assessment (PISA) . . . The results in these tests are simply not good enough. Nova Scotian students, parents and communities deserve better outcomes.*[8]

Although these test results were now being used as a primary reason to completely reform the system of educational governance, this was the entire extent of the discussion of the results. There was no evaluation in the Glaze report of how well Nova Scotia students had done, only the statement that they had not done well enough. As pointed out in previous chapters, an examination of these scores beyond the media sound-bites shows that students had done remarkably well in many areas. But the message of the report was that schools were failing and needed to undergo a serious reformation.

The evidence presented connecting student achievement to the proposed changes rested entirely on Glaze's belief system. She presented no data, no research, no theory as to how changes in governance would improve student achievement. Beyond her "strong" beliefs, there was no empirical evidence presented to suggest that her recommendations would make a difference in the academic achievement of Nova Scotia students.

The report made a total of twenty-two recommendations, which were organized across seven broad categories of benefits they would generate, or, as they were called in the report, catalysts.

These catalysts identified what would be accomplished if the report's recommendations were adopted. Among them: "Organize the system to focus on student learning and achievement" (reinforcing the idea that the current system was not set up to do so), "Make the system better for teachers and principals" and the oft-repeated reformist mantra "Increase trust, accountability and transparency."[9] Some of the recommendations were obvious and desirable, such as a suggestion that the responsibility for accounting and finance be taken off the plates of school principals and that the government develop a recruitment and retention strategy for teachers. But these amounted to little compared to the series of recommendations that rocked Nova Scotia's public education system.

The first recommendation was that all seven of the elected, English-language school boards in the province be eliminated. Instead of having what Glaze referred to as "disconnected silos," she suggested a model that would see all the power for making decisions transferred directly to a provincial body made up of the board superintendents, whose job titles would be changed to "regional executive directors of education." These individuals would report directly to the deputy minister and would ultimately be responsible and accountable for student achievement. It was also recommended that the role of the School Advisory Councils (SACs) be expanded.

Glaze had several criticisms of the elected boards. She pointed out that in a great many cases school-board elections were determined by acclamation, indicating public apathy toward the position. She also cited cases in Nova Scotia where various governments had found it necessary to take over certain functions of or, in some cases, entirely dismiss dysfunctional elected boards. Finally, she cited comments she had heard from contributors during her information gathering sessions, particularly the online survey. In response to the question "What changes should be made to the administration of school boards?" it was reported that 26 per cent of the respondents felt that boards should be cut, with a "large majority calling for either one for the entire province or two (one English, one French)."[10]

While it is true that there had been some dysfunction in elected school boards in Nova Scotia in recent years, as Glaze pointed out in her report, such difficulties are commonplace in school boards across the country. The trend of creating larger and larger school districts has led to school board members having more responsibility and having to be responsive to increasing numbers of parents and issues, while at the same time experiencing decreasing autonomy in decision making. Finally, according to the survey's own statistics, the call to cut school boards came from fewer than four hundred Nova Scotians — hardly a number to justify such a drastic change in school governance.

Despite the minister of education's assurances that the report was going to be created free of governmental influence, many saw this recommendation as evidence to the contrary. This idea of board elimination had been on the Liberal Party radar since April 2016, when a resolution was approved at the party's annual general meeting to eliminate English-language school boards. The argument for the elimination included a direct reference to work done by AIMS. In part, the resolution that suggested this change had read:

> WHEREAS as reported by Paul Bennett of Schoolhouse Consulting, "School board reduction or total elimination is on the public agenda as citizens see it as an obvious cost-saving measure. Regional or district school boards have become remote to most citizens and taxpayers . . . today's elected School Board trustees are basically limited to advocacy and 'rubber-stamping' monthly staff reports."[11]

This quote was taken from a report published by Bennett for AIMS in 2010, which also stated "Prominent conservative think tanks such as the Atlantic Institute for Market Studies

(AIMS) now favour replacing school boards with school advisory councils (SACs) vested with expanded powers."[12]

That this exact model, actively promoted by AIMS, was now being recommended by a supposed arms-length expert spoke of the extent to which the group and its ideology were influencing the narrative.

The negative impact of the abolition of school boards on public schools cannot be overstated. In her book *Reign of Error: The Hoax of the Privatization Movement and the Danger to America's Public Schools*, author and advocate Diane Ravitch summarizes the issue:

> *In the past decade, reformers have sought to centralize control over education policy so that the reforms they favor may be imposed without debate or delay. They say, "We can't wait." They argue that school boards are obstacles to speedy reform. . . . [T]hey want the freedom to open privately managed charter schools without having to take local opinion into account; they want the freedom to close public schools without listening to the parents or communities.*[13]

By adopting the stance that school boards were to be abolished, the Glaze report, and the Liberal government, were setting a dangerous precedent. In place of what was admittedly a slow and cumbersome democracy, they were proposing what would undoubtedly be a less cumbersome autocracy. This change effectively removed public voice from the conversation. Without duly elected school boards to represent a community vision of schools, there were very real questions to be asked about whether public education could still be considered "public." If AIMS were to realize their vision of an open-market education system in Nova Scotia, removing elected school boards eliminated a major impediment to that goal.

Further evidence of neoliberal thinking was the series of recommendations about teacher accountability. In her report, Glaze proposed that the province set up a provincial College of Educators, which would act as "an independent body to license, govern, discipline and regulate the teaching profession." Glaze wrote:

> *The College would perform some roles now held by the department, such as teacher certification, and by the NSTU, such as discipline ... an independent college of educators would be seen as impartial and without the conflict of interest when a group is in charge of both negotiating its membership needs and overseeing discipline.*[14]

But the NSTU did not hold the responsibility for disciplining teachers. The fact that Glaze repeated this erroneous claim and the related claim of conflict of interest gave critics further cause to doubt the integrity of the report.

This became even more problematic when Glaze used it to recommend that school principals and vice-principals be removed from the NSTU and given their own separate association. Glaze argued: "This model would establish a coherent management–educator model, instead of the conflict of interest that currently exists with both management and employee in the same union."[15] That this recommendation mirrored so closely the 2015 *Action Plan* and the earlier AIMS report only added fuel to the fire. When considered alongside the government's already established anti-union stance, this recommendation, contained in a report that was ostensibly about improving student achievement, seemed only to serve the goal of attacking the NSTU.

As if to emphasize this as an ultimate end, Glaze insisted that the principal organization should not be a separate bargaining unit within the NSTU. Instead, Glaze stated "this association would not be designed to be another union. It would be a professional association to enhance the profession and build public confidence."[16] Thus, administrators would be stripped of their collective bargaining rights and would be unable to participate in job action. It would also see the ranks of the NSTU reduced by about 10 per cent.

The Glaze report also made several recommendations about standardized testing, further aligning the document with neoliberal reforms. Using the argument that Nova Scotia's scores on international assessments were cause for alarm, the report suggested that the government set up an entirely new entity, separate from the Department of Education and Early Childhood Development, to create, administer and ensure alignment with standardized tests. This was, again, with the objective of improving the province's academic standing. In Glaze's words, when it came to such measures, "Nova Scotia students are not doing well enough; they are underperforming."[17]

Rather suddenly, a document materialized that encapsulated the neoliberal vision of what education should be. Here we had a report created by an outside consultant, based on the shaky premise that our schools were failing. The solutions proposed included an increased emphasis on teacher accountability, a larger focus on standardized testing and a concentrated attack on two of the entities standing in the way of the neoliberal reformists: the union and democratically elected school boards.

Not all the recommendations held within the Glaze report were damaging to the public education system. Some of the recommendations — such as calling on the government to develop a recruitment and retention plan for teachers and establishing a unit within the Department of Education to support immigrant families — were more than welcome and long overdue. However, the overall theme of the report was hard to ignore. The GERM ideas were now firmly embedded in Nova Scotian soil.

There was little opportunity for anyone in the province to weigh the pros and cons of the report. Using a political strategy known as a *blitzkrieg*, the Liberal government immediately embarked upon a well-planned and coordinated strategy to achieve its ends. The day after the Glaze report was publicly released, the minister of education announced that the government would be adopting all twenty-two recommendations contained in the report and would be moving forward immediately with eleven of them.[18] Among the eleven slated for immediate action were the most contentious. The NSTU would be weakened by the removal of administrators; a College of Teachers would be set up to increase teacher accountability practices; standardized testing would become a more important aspect of the education system; and the potential for local, elected officials to mount any sort of resistance to this, or any future educational reforms, would be destroyed by abolishing elected school boards.

Reaction to this announcement was swift and harsh. School board members, many of whom had met personally with Glaze, spoke of feeling betrayed by the decision to eliminate elected boards. Some members took to social media, pointing out that many of the reasons why Glaze had been critical of the bodies were being addressed. In 2015, the Nova Scotia auditor general had reviewed school-board operation in the province and had called attention to a number of issues, and boards were in the process of modifying their policies and practices to correct the shortcomings.

Board members also complained that many of the issues they had been struggling with came from provincial governmental interference, particularly the school review, closing and building process. This was most obvious when it came to new school construction, with the auditor general himself questioning some high-profile new school construction announcements in Liberal ridings. In some cases, the construction of these schools had gone against the wishes of the locally elected school board, who had been overridden by the minister. In an ironic twist to this story, Nova Scotia was slated to host the Canadian School Boards Association Congress in July 2018.[19]

Elected school board members were joined by representatives of the Black Educators Association (BEA) of Nova Scotia, who quickly panned Glaze's recommendations around African Nova Scotian students. Although Glaze had been critical of the way in which Nova Scotia was serving minority communities (based, again, on standardized test results), she had not consulted with the group on their view of the issues. The Glaze report also ignored the recommendations of the Black Learners Advisory Committee (BLAC) *Report on Education*, which had been created in 1994 and had served as a living document since that time. The BLAC report had served as a guide for dealing with racial inequity in the system and represented a vision of education for African Nova Scotian students that had been developed by the very community it served. In an interview with *Global News*, BEA president Karen Hudson asked "how can you do a report on African Nova Scotia communities and not reflect on historical documents that reflect who we are?"[20]

The loudest protests against the Glaze report came from teachers. Many were quick to draw the parallels between the recommendations of the Glaze report and the minister's *Action Plan* of 2015, and many were keenly aware of the fundamental flaws in the document. The suggestion that these measures would result in better student achievement seemed baseless, and nothing more than a way to sell the public on the idea. Furthermore, having a government accept every recommendation of a supposedly impartial consultant a mere twenty-four hours after a report had been publicly released was unprecedented and lent credence to the suspicion that the whole endeavour had been a game of smoke and mirrors. That the government chose to immediately implement the recommendations that best suited their political purposes left little doubt in the minds of many that this had been the intent all along.

Finally, and perhaps most damagingly, many of the changes closely mirrored the governance changes that had been legislated upon Ontario schools almost a decade earlier by the Conservative government of Mike Harris. These had included removing principals and vice-principals from their union, expanded provincial testing and a reduction in the number of school boards (although Harris did not go so far as to eliminate them). This new system of educational governance, which some have referred to as "radical centralization of decision making,"[21] and which was sold to the public as being specifically designed to meet the unique needs of one province, seemed simply a re-tooling of the Ontario model, which had itself been heavily influenced by neoliberal ideology.

To teachers on the ground, the report seemed a set of punitive measures resulting from the unrest of the previous two years and a way for the government to remove barriers to its agenda — a way for the government to accomplish what it could not during the collective bargaining process and without having to concern itself with public perception impacting an upcoming election.

Over the course of a few weeks, teachers mobilized in protest against the government's actions. The focus was the measures around standardized testing, the establishment of a College of Teachers and the removal of administrators from the NSTU. On the standardized testing issue, teachers were concerned that the establishment of this testing body would lead to an inordinate focus on literacy and numeracy skills for students and a connection between test scores and teacher evaluations. Indeed, one of Glaze's recommendations had specifically proposed tying professional development to student achievement, so it seemed not unreasonable to conclude that an "Americanized" system of teacher evaluation could be in the works.

When it came to the College of Teachers, there was more resistance. It was not so much that teachers objected to being held to a higher professional standard, but that the model being suggested was based on the Ontario model, which Glaze seemed to be holding up as an exemplar. This model had done little to improve education in that province, and, indeed, teachers were quite leery of a number of practices followed by the Ontario

College of Teachers, including publishing names of teachers who were facing disciplinary action but who had not yet had their cases heard. The fact that Glaze had suggested that membership in the college should include "substantial representation from business, labour, industry, and others, such as provincial parent groups and community organizations" added to the fire.[22] Suggesting that business and industry have a direct influence over the governance of teachers firmly aligned with the neoliberal agenda, and seemed a direct undermining of the professional autonomy of teachers.

There was also concern expressed around the removal of principals from the union, both from teachers and principals. Teachers were quick to point out that despite the way in which Glaze had framed the issue, having principals in the same union as teachers was the norm in more provinces than it was the exception. Where this was not the case, there was evidence of a marked uptick in labour unrest in terms of grievances filed against the department. Principals themselves were tremendously concerned and added their voices to the protests. Many were worried about the implications of working in schools without union protection and felt they were being used as political pawns. They had not asked to be removed from their union; they were being forced.

Considering the weak case presented to defend this idea, many principals also found themselves asking what purpose would be served by removing them from the NSTU. To reiterate, the NSTU was not responsible for disciplining teachers and the capacity for principals themselves to do so was extremely limited. Principals and vice-principals in Nova Scotia do not have the authority to dismiss or even to suspend teachers, and although they can discipline teachers, this discipline is very limited. This is because teachers are not employed by the principals, they are employed by the Regional Education Centres. If there are performance issues, the principal certainly has a role to play and the union ensures due process, but neither of these roles was likely to change in the new system.

Most importantly, there was the question of the impact on students. It was obvious to teachers that there was the potential for the relationship between teachers and their administration to become strained. Having just emerged from a contentious job action, teachers were concerned about schools developing a "management versus employee" mentality, and that the working environment could become toxic. There was evidence that this had been the case after principals had been removed from their bargaining units in Ontario.

Probably the most egregious aspect of the recommended changes for teachers was that they were happening outside the collective bargaining process. Many, including the removal of administrators from the union, would require not only changes to the provincial Teachers' Professional Agreement (TPA) and the regional agreements, but also amendments to the *Education Act* itself. The *Act* had long been considered sacrosanct, and traditionally, changes to the TPA (much like any contract) would require both sides to come to an agreement. However, the Glaze recommendations were made without any consultation or discussion with the union. Essentially, the government was going to rewrite the teachers' contract, a contract that they themselves had imposed on teachers only a few months earlier. For many teachers, this represented yet another betrayal and an abject abuse of power. If the government could rewrite the contract as it suited them, what value was there in a contract in the first place?

Teachers, parents and advocates once again took to social media, this time to blast the Glaze report. Public meetings were organized where teachers explained to the public the flaws of the report and exposed it as a political tool. The NSTU organized a series of petition-signing events, and MLAs were once again inundated with calls and emails insisting that the adoption of the Glaze recommendations at least be slowed, allowing some time to consider the potential impact on students. What was lost on the leadership of the NSTU, however, was that slowing down to consider the implications of the report is what a *blitzkrieg* is undertaken to avoid. A political *blitzkrieg*, by its very nature, is intended to keep the opposition off-balance and overwhelm their defenses, and the swiftness with which the government was moving forward with their reforms had caught everyone off guard.

The government refused to deviate from their path; they were not even open to the idea of holding discussions with the NSTU. In a desperate, last-ditch effort to slow the implementation, the union called for an illegal strike vote as a means of getting the government to hear their concerns. On February 21, 2018, it was announced that an astonishing 83 per cent of Nova Scotia teachers were willing to illegally walk off the job and face fines to halt the report.[23]

Even in the face of this threat, the government remained obstinate. Although the minister of education did say he was open to meeting with the NSTU and would perhaps "show some flexibility," he went on to say that his government would not be slowing implementation. When asked about this possibility at a news conference, the minister replied, "We do need to move forward with reform. Our kids can't wait," using the FUD tactic to his advantage. The premier also said that his government would not compromise on the Glaze report. Using the threat of an illegal strike as leverage, NSTU leadership did get a meeting with the government, but failed to convince them to delay the legislation. They did get some compromises, in particular a temporary abandonment of the plan to develop a College of Teachers and a centralized assessment department. Finally, although they were unable to keep principals and vice-principals as part of the NSTU, those individuals could retain an "affiliation" with the union, which would at least provide them some measure of protection. On March 1, 2018, the NSTU Provincial Executive announced that the government had "done enough" to avoid an illegal walkout.[24] That same day, Bill 72, *The Education Reform Act*, was introduced into the House, and within a few days, was passed into law.[25]

Thus, in less than six months, the government had used its majority status and a political *blitzkrieg* to centralize the education authority, abolish locally elected school boards and eviscerate the collective bargaining process. To put a final stamp on its ultimate authority, Bill 72 increased the fines that would be imposed on the NSTU for holding an illegal strike from $10,000 per day to $100,000.

Although there was relief on the part of some teachers around the compromises achieved, it was hard for many to see this moment as anything other than another staggering defeat. Even though it was obvious that this government would not be moved, many teachers felt, rightly or wrongly, that giving up on the walkout represented a complete capitulation. This undoubtedly contributed to the defeat of incumbent President Liette Doucet during the May 2018 NSTU presidential election.

So there you have it. An ideology born in a small town in Switzerland and invigorated in the United States during the Space Race of the 1960s made its way across the globe, spread like an infection and finally reached Nova Scotia's relatively isolated shores. It had taken the threat of an illegal strike to slow down the full-fledged adoption of the neoliberal-based GERM ideas of high-stakes testing and higher accountability measures for teachers, but it had been a pyrrhic victory. The cost for the union, and the teachers who made up its ranks, had been incredibly high. And although the rate had been slowed, for those of us in the field, it was perfectly clear that the infection was still spreading.

The legislation of a provincial contract, the removal of principals from the NSTU and the abolition of elected school boards can only be seen as resounding victories for the neoliberal reformists. With those wins accomplished, they will now turn their attention to other aspects of the system that stand in the way of their ultimate goal. We can expect a new regime of standardized testing and more accountability practices for teachers, as well as a continued push for privatized charter schools. The attack on the public education system is multi-pronged. And the neoliberal advocates at the think tanks are nothing if not patient.

Using their capacity to manipulate popular media, the reformists will repeat their message, perhaps for decades, until people come to believe what they are saying makes sense. Once this becomes the case, they will only require a government that supports their ideology. Then their vision of a privatized, for-profit education system could be fully realized, and the days of a publicly funded, publicly controlled education system would become the stuff of legend.

The question that remains for all of us who support a different view of public education is: What can be done to stop them?

CHAPTER 10
How Can We Defend Public Education in Nova Scotia?

In the Introduction, I suggested that Nova Scotia is, in many ways, the perfect petri dish for educational reformism. That it took the threat of an illegal strike by the province's teachers to slow the reformists shows the extraordinary power of the movement and how ripe the province has been for the picking.

I have painted a rather dystopian picture of the last twenty-five or so years of change, and I feel I should soften that a bit. Nova Scotia's schools are staffed with what I believe are world-class educators, and my experience has been that the same can be said of the people who staff the Department of Education. Indeed, I believe that one of the strengths of our system and its internal leadership is how well we have survived the constant pressure of those who would privatize our system. I must also allow that when a new policy is enacted that mirrors the neoliberal worldview, it may not be that those in charge are out to permit a corporate takeover of our schools.

Yet, as the years have passed, even the best-intentioned educational leaders have found themselves under intense pressure to conform to the developing view of public education.

When the public raises a hue and cry for such things as higher accountability measures for teachers, and when newspapers are full of reports about low test scores, action is not just expected, it is required.

I am also keenly aware that the notion of a global movement working to influence public opinion and seize control of our education system reads like science fiction, but it is this ability to operate under the radar that makes the workings of groups like Atlas and Fraser so effective. And they are not alone. There are many respected individuals, both public and private, who firmly believe our education systems can only be improved by implementing more stringent accountability practices and free-market solutions.

When writing about the prevalence of socialist thought in 1947, Hayek explained that the intellectuals who were promoting socialism were not doing so purely for selfish interests nor with evil intentions. He allowed that it was mostly good will, good intentions and honest convictions that were driving the ideology. And as much as I may disagree with them, I recognize that, as with any movement of this magnitude, there are those within the neoliberal camp who are undoubtedly well intentioned.

It is not that the reformists do not want children to succeed, rather it is how they define that success. In a neoliberal framework, being the best math student in your school or having the highest test scores in the region is the ultimate goal. However, that approach sets up a troubling framework of winners and losers. It is a framework that inherently values individual gains over the collective good and operates on the illusion that all children have an equal chance of crossing the finish line first.

It is also a framework that values the accumulation of personal wealth and property as a key factor in achieving individual freedom. When taken to the extreme, this allows for a lapse in some fundamental moral guidelines. Many of the charter school scandals and failures in the US have resulted from this "profit at all costs" approach. If we allow ourselves to be convinced that we should model our entire education system on these same ideals, how can we possibly anticipate a different outcome? Anyone who saw their retirement savings evaporate during the financial crash of 2008 can attest to the dangers of allowing neoliberal, free-market policies to run free. If the Lehman Brothers financial empire can collapse almost overnight, what makes us think that our schools would not be similarly susceptible? How can we educate children about teamwork, cooperation or altruism if our guiding principles are based on an individualistic world view?

Perhaps I am naïve, but I believe that public education is, ultimately, about achieving a public good. It is not about increasing test scores or about more accountability or turning a profit. In its purest form, public education is about giving all citizens, regardless of background or socio-economic status or ethnicity, the tools to create meaningful lives. To raise themselves up. To challenge their own belief systems and the belief systems of others. To speak up. To be heard. To be valued members of society. It is about teaching a rich, broad curriculum that is culturally relevant. The system and the people who work within it consistently strive to achieve these goals, working collaboratively and collectively to get better at what they do. They share resources and strategies and ideas with the intention of developing schools that will work for everyone, not just a chosen few.

Public education is a public institution, and it has been public dissatisfaction with the system that has ultimately been fuelling the call for change. This raises the question of what factors make people so receptive to the largely unsupported claims that schools are failing and that there is an urgent need for immediate implementation of the measures packaged up in the GERM solution. The main reason is simple. People believe that our schools are failing because there is no one out there making the case that they are not.

Hayek himself used a very similar argument for why socialism had taken hold in the early part of the twentieth century. He explained that the socialists had been able to provide a vision of the future that was not the status quo. This "utopian view" was what, according to Hayek, had drawn intellectuals toward socialism in the first place and was what was needed in order to advance the libertarian movement. When it comes to education, those who would criticize our system in order to tear it down have gained such ground because there is little corresponding counter-narrative. It is the neoliberals who are providing the utopian view of how education can be reformed. There is little effort from any side to truly advance and promote the cause of public education, to celebrate its successes and to validate its achievements. If public education is to survive as an institution, it needs some advocacy.

Who should shoulder that burden? If advocacy and promotion are necessary to ensure control of one of our major public institutions to remain in the hands of the public and not become a private, for-profit enterprise, who should take up that task?

I suggest, at the risk of sounding trite, that we all have a part to play.

To start with, there is a responsibility for advocacy that falls to teacher organizations, and in Nova Scotia that means the NSTU. All unions have the power to affect tremendous social change and are ultimately established to better the circumstances of their members, and of the working class in general. If the union truly believes it exists to "advance quality public education," as its mission statement says, it can no longer do so quietly in the background. It must not be perceived as emerging only in times of conflict, but rather it must work to advance the truth that the union is made up of individual teachers — teachers who positively impact students and communities at a fundamental level.

Anti-unionists have an insatiable desire and uncanny ability to portray unions as self-serving. Unionized fights for better wages and working conditions are misrepresented as fat-cat union brass working only to line their own pockets and well-paid union members trying to raise their salaries and extend their benefits far beyond what they deserve. As a union leader myself, I can tell you that there is no money in it, at least not as far as the NSTU is concerned. However, if the public does not know any better, if they are not informed, if unions like mine spend no time informing the public of what it is we do, then the anti-unionists will always have the upper hand. It is much easier for think tanks to vilify unions if there is no counter-narrative offered.

Within our communities I see another significant source of advocacy. In many jurisdictions across North America, groups of concerned and informed parents have banded together to lobby against the neoliberal movement. In the US, organizations such as the Network for Public Education have fought with great success at a grassroots level to expose the underlying threat posed by the charter-school movement. They have been joined by church leaders who have formed associations such as Pastors for Children to support local, publicly funded schools. In Canada, groups like People for Education in Ontario, under the direction of Annie Kidder, have been lobbying government since the mid-1990s for a strong, publicly funded education system.

In Nova Scotia, similar organizations are materializing, although most are in their infancy. Groups such as Educators for Social Justice and Nova Scotia Parents for Public Education (Parents4PublicED) emerged from the ashes of the 2015–18 conflict. As they continue to gather steam, there is potential for them to have a significant impact on ensuring future governments do not continue down the road to privatization.

If grassroots movements are to be successful, however, they need support. It requires that individuals take the time to get involved. In the same way that the NSTU cannot simply appear for contract negotiations, public push-back cannot be limited to the traditional "Save Our Schools" efforts that crop up from time to time. People need to engage outside of times of crisis, to attend meetings and to get informed in order to push back.

Although there is tremendous potential in community-based activism, one of the only Canadian organizations that has an immediate capacity to create a counter-narrative against the neoliberal creep is the Ottawa-based Canadian Centre for Policy Alternatives (CCPA). Decidedly left-leaning in its politics, the CCPA has long been pushing back against the false narrative of failing schools and corporatization, as evidenced in Chapter 2 of *Class Warfare*. However, when it comes to political clout and funding, the CCPA is dwarfed by its right-wing counterparts.

According to Canada Revenue Agency documents, in 2017 AIMS paid out $360,000 in salaries and benefits alone and $100,000 in consulting fees,[1] presumably to authors like Paul Bennett and Michael Zwaagstra. In the same year, the total budget of the Nova Scotia office of the CCPA was less than $100,000. Its lone employee earned $66,000.

With the recent merger of The Fraser Institute and AIMS, the potential resources available to expand a regional neoliberal agenda have grown significantly. As mentioned in Chapter 1, for the year ending December 31, 2017, The Fraser Institute registered revenues of $11 million,[2] with $5 million of that coming from other charities, presumably those associated with the Atlas Network. (The Fraser Institute home page boasts that it has "ties to a global network of think tanks in 87 countries."[3])

Although at the time of publication it was unclear why the merger took place, The Fraser Institute declared in a press release in late 2019 that the end result was the creation of Canada's largest "independent think tank".[4] Whether AIMS will survive this merger in its present form or will be restructured to suit the needs of the more right-wing Fraser Institute is yet to be determined. However, the addition of their substantial war chest in the fight to promote free-market solutions in Atlantic Canada may prove a significant development.

Supporting the research and publishing efforts of the CCPA is another avenue available for concerned citizens who wish to counter that move, particularly if they want to see control of public education remain in the public realm.

Then there is the role that must be played by the fourth estate — the mainstream media. Authors Maude Barlow and Heather-

Jane Robertson reported that even in 1991 teachers were among the least likely groups to be quoted in stories about the education system, and little has changed since that time. Some of the responsibility for this missing voice must be laid at the feet of the union, which has often discouraged teachers from speaking directly to the media.

The absence of teachers willing to speak on the subject of education should not, however, give a free pass to the press to arbitrarily assign expertise to consultants who work outside the system. Given the current state of the news media, journalists have a greater responsibility than ever to examine the source of their information. Although finding a spokesperson from AIMS to weigh in on the subject of public education may prove expedient, doing so without exploring the motivation behind the views, or perhaps examining the accuracy of their claims, is irresponsible. There remains a certain authority in stories that come from mainstream media outlets in Canada. As a result, the capacity they have to do lasting damage by repeating poorly researched, and sometimes completely inaccurate, claims of school failure is considerable.

Finally, when it comes to the preservation of public education, the organization with the greatest capacity for impact is, by far, our government. Governments do not spend much time or money promoting the system they themselves have built.

It would be easy to blame this silence on the fact that our current government is decidedly neoliberal. But successive governments in Nova Scotia have fallen victim to the same line of thinking. Even when the ruling party was not dominated by neoliberal discourse, there was little effort to promote or celebrate public education.

If this were a private entity, they would be trumpeting this system to the skies. They would be celebrating their own innovations, positioning themselves as a mover and a shaker, singing the praises of their hard-working and innovative workforce. All this would be done with an eye to drawing consumers to the product. This could allow jurisdictions like ours to become veritable education destinations. Yet, from governments across the country, we hear crickets.

Instead of looking at ways of promoting the system, politicians have, time and again, used education as a political tool, painting their all-too-familiar reforms as a way of repairing the perceived failures of previous governments. When the status quo is called into question, it is much easier to offer alternatives than to defend the current model. Unfortunately for public education, often the only alternative models readily available are those that are firmly rooted in neoliberal soil.

Furthermore, addressing the underlying issues of a system such as education is not only more difficult, but more time consuming and expensive than offering an alternative to the status quo. If standardized tests results are not up to snuff, it is far easier for governments to, say, increase accountability measures for teachers than it is to address underlying issues such as child poverty or racial inequality.

Although Nova Scotia is a relatively small province, when it comes to education, we punch well above our weight. It is here that our most valuable resource lies. Not in our oceans. Not in our forests. Not in our blueberry fields or in our apple orchards. It lies within our classrooms. We have the educational expertise and the infrastructure. It is high time we stopped being a model of educational reformism gone awry and time we started to recognize and promote ourselves as what we long have been: a model of educational excellence.

I can't help but wonder how much further ahead we would be as a province if twenty-five years ago we had committed to a collectivist vision of public education as opposed to pursuing the neoliberal one. If all the money and time spent on such endeavours as *Horizons*, the *Action Plan* and the Glaze report had gone into promoting and enhancing what we were doing well, as opposed to what the neoliberals wanted us to believe we were doing poorly, would we still be languishing as one of Canada's "have-not" provinces?

There is nothing but a lack of political will stopping us from becoming another Finland: a region with an education system that others, indeed entire countries, aspire to. But for that to happen, all of us, union, government, media and the public, both individually and collectively, must accept one single, solitary truth.

Our schools are not underperforming. They are under attack.

And unless we stop placidly accepting the messaging of Fear, Uncertainty and Doubt being advanced by the neoliberals, control of one of the last, most fundamental public entities in our possession will slip, quietly and forever, away from our collective grasp.

Acknowledgements

Thank you to Formac Publishing and my editor Kara Turner. As well, a special thank you to Pamela Rogers for her research. Finally, I would be remiss if I did not offer a reverent, heartfelt acknowledgement to all the amazing people who stand shoulder to shoulder with teachers to advance the cause of public education in our province.

References

Introduction

1. Ryan Gibson, Joanne Fitzgibbons, and Nina R. Nunez, "Nova Scotia," in *State of Rural Canada* (Canadian Rural Revitalization Foundation, 2015), sorc.crrf.ca/ns/.
2. Jelmer Evers and René Kneyber, eds., *Flip The System: Changing Education from the Ground Up* (London: Routledge, 2015).

Chapter 1

1. Kathryn Blaze Carlson, "Math Wars: The Division over How to Improve Test Scores," *Globe and Mail*, January 14, 2014, https://tgam.ca/33SkEYY.
2. Bruce. J. Caldwell, s.v. "F.A. Hayek," in *Encyclopedia Britannica*, last modified May 4, 2019, www.britannica.com/biography/F-A-Hayek.
3. F.A. Hayek, "The Intellectuals and Socialism," in *The Intellectuals: A Controversial Portrait*, ed. George B. de Huszar, (Glencoe, IL: The Free Press, 1960), 371–84, https://mises.org/library/intellectuals-and-socialism-0
4. Donald Gutstein, *Harperism: How Stephen Harper and His Think Tank Colleagues Have Transformed Canada* (Toronto: James Lorimer and Company, Ltd., 2014).
5. "Global Directory," Atlas Network, accessed May, 2019, www.atlasnetwork.org/partners/global-directory.
6. Atlas Network, "Form 990," in *Annual Report 2017*, accessed May, 2019, http://bit.ly/2TSuG7W.
7. "Our Story," Atlas Network, accessed May, 2019, www.atlasnetwork.org/about/our-story.
8. Wikipedia, s.v. "Antony Fisher," last modified November 22, 2018. en.wikipedia.org/wiki/Antony_Fisher.
9. Beth Hong, "Charitable Fraser Institute Received $4.3 Million in Foreign Funding since 2000," *Vancouver Observer*, August 30, 2012, http://bit.ly/2KNV93t.

10. Daphne Bramham, "Lessons for Canada from How the Koch Brothers Hijacked Democracy," *Vancouver Sun*, September 25, 2016, http://bit.ly/3OohuKo.
11. Donald Gutstein, "Follow the Money, Part 1 — The Weston Family," Rabble.ca, March 25, 2014, http://bit.ly/2KMxvEy.
12. Canada Revenue Agency, "Detailed Financial Information — The Fraser Institute," last modified October 23, 2017, http://bit.ly/2zgrQA2.
13. Fraser Institute, *Canada's Most Influential Think Tank: 2017 Annual Report*, http://bit.ly/2Zbl3qL.
14. Gutstein, *Harperism*.

Chapter 2

1. Wikipedia, s.v. "Sputnik 1," last modified February 6, 2019. en.wikipedia.org/wiki/Sputnik_1.
2. "Sputnik 1," NASA Space Science Data Coordinated Archive, accessed May, 2019, https://go.nasa.gov/2PbV24h.
3. Andrew Glass, "Reagan Fires 11,000 Striking Air Traffic Controllers, Aug. 5, 1981," *Politico*, August 5, 2017, https://politi.co/2TTIe30.
4. Donald Gutstein, *Harperism: How Stephen Harper and His Think Tank Colleagues Have Transformed Canada* (Toronto: James Lorimer and Company Ltd., 2014), 84–85.
5. Milton Friedman, "The Role of Government in Education," in *Economics and the Public Interest*, ed. Robert A. Solo (New Brunswick, NJ: Rutgers University Press, 1955), http://bit.ly/2ZtBjD6.
6. Ibid.
7. Ibid.
8. National Commission on Excellence in Education, *A Nation at Risk: The Imperative for Educational Reform*, 1983, http://bit.ly/2Zgwngt.
9. Ibid., "Introduction."
10. Ibid., "Introduction."
11. Ibid.

12. William G. Spady, *Outcome-Based Education: Critical Issues and Answers* (Arlington, VA: American Association of School Administrators, 1994), files.eric.ed.gov/fulltext/ED380910.pdf.
13. "History," Organisation for Economic Co-operation and Development (OECD), accessed May, 2019, www.oecd.org/about/history/.
14. "About: PISA," OECD, accessed May, 2019, www.oecd.org/pisa/aboutpisa/.
15. Jack Lyne, "Who's No. 1? Finland, Japan and Korea, Says OECD Education Study," *Site Selection*, December 10, 2001, http://bit.ly/2Zm9tED.
16. Andrew Rudalevige, "The Politics of No Child Left Behind," *Education Next* 3, no. 4 (2003), www.educationnext.org/the-politics-of-no-child-left-behind/.
17. White House, "Race to the Top," obamawhitehouse.archives.gov/issues/education/k-12/race-to-the-top.
18. Maude Barlow and Heather-Jane Robertson, *Class Warfare: The Assault on Canada's Schools* (Toronto: Key Porter Books, 1994).
19. Tom Fennell, "What's Wrong at School?" *Maclean's*, January 11, 1993, http://bit.ly/30qVP4p.
20. Atlantic Provinces Education Foundation, *The Atlantic Canada Framework for Essential Graduation Learnings* (Halifax: Atlantic Provinces Education Foundation, 1996), http://bit.ly/2LfA1Cz.
21. This wording appears in every foundation document, an example of which can be viewed here: www.ed.gov.nl.ca/edu/k12/curriculum/documents/art/arts_found.pdf on page 5.
22. Nova Scotia Teachers Union, *Taking Time to Reflect: The NSTU Response to the Atlantic Canada Graduation Outcomes* (Halifax: Nova Scotia Teachers Union, 1994).

Chapter 3

1. Pasi Sahlberg, *Finnish Lessons: What Can the World Learn from Educational Change in Finland?* (New York: Teachers College Press, 2010).
2. Ibid., 99.
3. Ibid., 101.

4. Ibid.
5. Andy Hargreaves and Dennis Shirley, *The Fourth Way: The Inspiring Future for Educational Change* (Corwin, ON: Ontario Principal's Council and the National Staff Development Council, 2009).
6. Ibid., 11.
7. Erin Pottie, "Cape Breton Elementary Schools Losing Library Technicians," *Cape Breton Post*, May 31, 2018, http://bit.ly/31VWLhk.
8. Ontario Library Association, *School Libraries and Student Achievement in Ontario*, (Toronto: Ontario Library Association, 2006), 4, http://bit.ly/31ZKAA3.
9. Keith Curry Lance and Debra E. Kachel, "Why School Librarians Matter: What Years of Research Tell Us," *Phi Delta Kappan* 99, no. 7 (2018), 15–20.
10. Jonathan D. Ostry, Prakash Loungani and Davide Fourceri, "Neoliberalism: Oversold?" *Finance & Development* 53, no. 2 (June 2016), http://bit.ly/2NoZSdS.
11. Ibid.
12. Brian M. Stecher, et al. *Intensive Partnerships for Effective Teaching Enhanced How Teachers Are Evaluated but Had Little Effect on Student Outcomes* (Santa Monica, CA: RAND Corporation, 2018), www.rand.org/pubs/research_briefs/RB10009.html.
13. Ibid.

Chapter 4

1. Pamela Rogers, "Tracing Neoliberal Governmentality in Education: Disentangling Economic Crises, Accountability, and the Disappearance of Social Studies" (PhD diss., University of Ottawa, 2018).
2. Paul McCormick, *Conflict and Collegiality, The Nova Scotia Teachers Union, 1984–2012* (Halifax: Nova Scotia Teachers Union, 2012).
3. Government of Nova Scotia, Department of Education, *Restructuring Nova Scotia's Education System: Preparing All*

Students for a Lifetime of Learning (Halifax: Government of Nova Scotia, 1994).
4. Government of Nova Scotia, Department of Education, *Education Horizons: White Paper on Restructuring the Education System* (Halifax: Government of Nova Scotia, 1995).
5. Rogers, "Tracing Neoliberal Governmentality," 70–71.
6. Ibid., 70–74.
7. Ibid., 76.
8. Ibid., 78.
9. McCormick, *Conflict and Collegiality*, 129–30.
10. Early Learning and Education, *Learning for Life II: Brighter Futures Together* (Halifax: Department of Education, 2005), http://bit.ly/2Eh8ygJ
11. Alison Taylor, "'Re-culturing' Students and Selling Futures: School to Work Policy in Ontario," *Journal of Education and Work* 18, no. 3 (2005), 321–340.
12. Rogers, "Tracing Neoliberal Governmentality," 84.
13. Ibid., 82.
14. Department of Education, "Ten New Schools Authorized to Offer International Baccalaureate Program," press release, April 23, 2007, novascotia.ca/news/release/?id=20070423001.
15. Fred Genesee and Kathryn Lindholm-Leary, "Dual Language Education in Canada and the USA," in *Encyclopedia of Language and Education*, eds. Jim Cummins and Nancy Hornberger (Norwell, MA: Springer, 2007), 5:253–266, www.psych.mcgill.ca/perpg/fac/genesee/21.pdf.
16. Canadian Parents for French, *French as a Second Language Enrolment Statistics 2012–2013 to 2016–2017* (Ottawa: Canadian Parents for French, 2018), cpf.ca/en/files/Enrolement-Stats-2018-web-1.pdf.
17. Mary G. O'Brien, *Literature Review on the Impact of Second-Language Learning* (2017), http://bit.ly/2ZgaiCZ.
18. Fred Genesee and Kathryn Lindholm-Leary, "Dual Language Education in Canada and the USA," in *Encyclopedia of Language and Education*, 2nd ed., eds. Jim Cummins and Nancy Hornberger (Boston, MA: Springer, 2008), 5:253–266. http://bit.ly/36f48CS

19. Aaron Hutchins, "Just Say 'Non': The Problem with French Immersion," *Maclean's*, March 22, 2015. www.macleans.ca/education/just-say-non-the-problem-with-french-immersion/.
20. Rogers, "Tracing Neoliberal Governmentality," 84.
21. Rogers, "Tracing Neoliberal Governmentality."
22. Ibid., 164.
23. Ibid., 116.
24. Ibid., 117.
25. Ibid., 119–20.
26. Ibid.
27. Ibid., 125.
28. Ibid., 126.
29. Ibid., 127.
30. Ibid., 129.
31. Ibid., 128.

Chapter 5

1. "Welcome to the Fraser Institute," Fraser Institute, 2019, www.fraserinstitute.org/about.
2. Fred McMahon, *Looking the Gift Horse in the Mouth: The Impact of Federal Transfers on Atlantic Canada* (Halifax: Atlantic Institute for Market Studies, 1996).
3. "About Us," AIMS, 2017, www.aims.ca/about-us-2/.
4. Ibid.
5. Stephen Kimber, "The World According to John," *Atlantic Business*, December 19, 2013, www.atlanticbusinessmagazine.net/?article=the-world-according-to-john.
6. Angela MacIvor, "Dalhousie University Defends Fronting Money to 'Nova Scotia's Elite,'" *CBC*, August 18, 2016, www.cbc.ca/news/canada/nova-scotia/nova-scotia-leaders-mit-business-elite-dalhousie-province-1.3726515.
7. Valerie Strauss, "To Trump's Education Pick, the U.S. School System Is a 'Dead End.'" *Washington Post*, December 21, 2016, https://wapo.st/2Zpt5eQ.
8. Network for Public Education, *Charters and Consequences: An Investigative Series* (New York: Network for Public Education,

2017), 1, http://bit.ly/30lplbH.
9. Center for Research on Education Outcomes (CREDO), *National Chart School Study* (Stanford, CA: CREDO, 2013), https://stanford.io/2L05UPg.
10. Institute of Education Sciences, *The Evaluation of Charter School Impacts* (Washington, DC: U.S. Department of Education, 2010), http://bit.ly/2TVzY2H.
11. "KIPP DC INC, Form 990," ProPublica Nonprofit Explorer, 2017, http://bit.ly/33Smvgo.
12. Ibid.
13. Mark Binelli, "Michigan Gambled on Charter Schools. Its Children Lost," *New York Times*, September 5, 2017, www.nytimes.com/2017/09/05/magazine/michigan-gambled-on-charter-schools-its-children-lost.html.
14. Network for Public Education, "#AnotherDayAnotherCharterScandal," networkforpubliceducation.org/another-day-another-charter-scandal/.
15. Valerie Strauss, "Dark Money Just Keeps on Coming in School Board Races," *Washington Post*, October 29, 2017, https://wapo.st/2ROUqmT.
16. *Dark Money*, directed by Kimberly Reed, 2018, www.darkmoneyfilm.com.
17. National Center for the Study of Privatization in Education, Teachers College, Columbia University, ncspe.tc.columbia.edu/.
18. Atlantic Institute for Market Studies (AIMS), *Charter Schools in Atlantic Canada* (Halifax: AIMS, 1997), www.aims.ca/books-papers/charter-schools-in-atlantic-canada/.
19. Ibid., Section 4.
20. Donald Gutstein, "Follow the Money, Part 3: Big Oil and Calgary's School of Public Policy," Rabble.ca, April 8, 2014, http://bit.ly/2Hl8kHj.
21. Michael C. Zwaagstra, Rodney A. Clifton and John C. Long, *Getting the Fox Out of the Schoolhouse: How the Public Can Take Back Public Education* (Halifax: AIMS, 2007), aims.wpengine.com/site/media/aims/TakeBack.pdf.

22. Ibid., 1.
23. Ibid., 1.
24. Ibid., 32–33.

Chapter 6

1. Francis Willick, "Parents Weary of Report Card 'Mumbo-Jumbo,'" *The Chronicle Herald*, July 3, 2013.
2. Marc Montgomery, "Parents Giving Low Grades to Some School Report Cards," *Radio Canada International*, July 3, 2013, http://bit.ly/2KN09FK.
3. Bob Murphy, "'Bird Course' Adds Thousands of Dollars to Teachers' Pay," *CBC News*, February 19, 2014, http://bit.ly/30sdecO.
4. Ibid.
5. "Drake University Classes Banned as Upgrade for N.S. Teachers," *CBC News*, April 15, 2014, http://bit.ly/2ZnWXnP.
6. Ibid.
7. Marilla Stephenson, "Karen Casey, We're Broke in Case You Didn't Notice," *The Chronicle Herald*, April 30, 2014.
8. "Casey Should Rethink Drake," Editorial, *The Chronicle Herald*, May 3, 2014.
9. Bill Black, "Teacher-Centric Upgrades Could Cost over $50 Million," *The Chronicle Herald*, 2014.
10. Paul W. Bennett, "Lost Learning Time; Blizzard Bags' for Smart Snow Days," *The Chronicle Herald*, February 25, 2015.
11. Jean Laroche, "Karen Casey Open to Saturday Classes to Make up for Lost Storm Days," *CBC News*, February 27, 2015, www.cbc.ca/amp/1.2973583.
12. Government of Nova Scotia, Education and Early Childhood Development, "Minister Announces Changes to Support Teacher Excellence," March 3, 2015, novascotia.ca/news/release/?id=20150303004.
13. Ibid.
14. Michael Gorman, "Province Could Pay $7.5M for Cancelling Controversial Teacher Upgrades," *CBC News*, May 2, 2019, http://bit.ly/2ZeLITL.

15. Paul W. Bennett and Karen Mitchell, *Maintaining "Spotless Records": Professional Standards, Teacher Misconduct and the Teaching Profession* (Halifax: AIMS, 2014), http://bit.ly/2P5sfA6.
16. Ibid.
17. Ibid.
18. Ibid.
19. Ibid.
20. Frances Willick, "AIMS Teacher Report Gets Low Marks," *The Chronicle Herald*, March 21, 2014.
21. Caroline Alphonso, "Canada's Fall in Math-Education Ranking Sets off Alarm Bells," *Globe and Mail*, December 3, 2013, https://tgam.ca/3ooKl1n.
22. Dana Flavelle, "CEO Group Issues Call to Action on Skills Gap," *Toronto Star*, November 28, 2013, http://bit.ly/2L5272W.
23. Business Council of Canada, thebusinesscouncil.ca/.
24. Government of Nova Scotia, Department of Education and Early Childhood Development, "Nova Scotia Students Perform Well in International Assessments," December 3, 2013, novascotia.ca/news/release/?id=20131203001.
25. Frances Willick, "N.S. Students Slip in International Math Test," *The Chronicle Herald*, December 3, 2013.
26. Council of Ministers of Education, Canada (CMEC), *Measuring Up: Canadian Results of the OECD PISA Study* (Toronto: CMEC, 2013), http://bit.ly/2NoFtWk.
27. CMEC, *PCAP 2013: Report on the Pan-Canadian Assessment of Science, Reading, and Mathematics* (Toronto: CMEC, 2014), http://bit.ly/2zgWIRa.
28. "N.S. Students Doing Better in Math but Not up to National Average," *CBC News*, October 7, 2014, http://bit.ly/2ZtCHFO.
29. Frances Willick and Michael Gorman, "Middling Results for Nova Scotia Grade 8 Students on Canada-Wide Test," *The Chronicle Herald*, October 7, 2014.
30. "Latest Education Assessment Shows Nova Scotia Students Heading to 'New, Lower Plateau,'" *Truro News*, October 18, 2014, http://bit.ly/31Y6C6t.

Chapter 7

1. "Ontario Imposes Contracts on Public School Teachers," *CBC News*, January 3, 2013, http://bit.ly/2Zll62u.
2. "N.S. Teachers Slam Dexter's Education Cuts," *CBC News*, May 18, 2012, http://bit.ly/2Hf8qQD.
3. Nova Scotia Teachers Union (NSTU), "Education Partner Calls for Increased Funding," *The Teacher* 47, no. 5 (2012), nstu.ca/images/The%20Teacher/Maylayout2012TT.pdf.
4. Jane Taber, "Liberals Win Majority in N.S. Election," *Globe and Mail*, October 9, 2013, https://tgam.ca/2TWTITf.
5. Canadian Press, "Nova Scotia to Launch Major Public-Education Review," *Globe and Mail*, May 12, 2014, https://tgam.ca/2HyHOKH.
6. Peter Greene, "What Went Wrong with Teach for America," Progressive.org, February 17, 2016, progressive.org/public-school-shakedown/went-wrong-teach-america/.
7. "Board of Directors: Kyle Hill," Teach for Canada, 2017, teachforcanada.ca/en/staff/kyle-hill/.
8. "Who's Reviewing Nova Scotia's Education System?" *No Need to Raise Your Hand*, March 2, 2014, http://bit.ly/2HgUS76.
9. Department of Education and Early Childhood Development, *Disrupting the Status Quo: Nova Scotians Demand a Better Future for Every Student* (Halifax: Government of Nova Scotia, 2014), http://bit.ly/2zgWVUs.
10. Ibid., 3.
11. Ibid., 11.
12. Ibid., 22.
13. Ibid., 23.
14. Ibid., 27.
15. Ibid., 28.
16. Ibid., 31.
17. Ibid.
18. Department of Education and Early Childhood Development, *The 3 Rs: Renew, Refocus, Rebuild: Nova Scotia's Action Plan for Education 2015* (Halifax: Government of Nova Scotia, 2015), www.ednet.ns.ca/docs/educationactionplan2015en.pdf.

Chapter 8

1. Jane Taber, "Liberals Win Majority in N.S. Election," *Globe and Mail*, October 8, 2013, https://tgam.ca/2TWTITf.
2. Jean Laroche, "Premier Stephen McNeil's History with Labour Unions," *CBC News*, October 26, 2016, http://bit.ly/2ZgAIjX.
3. Bill No. 37, *Essential Health and Community Services Act*, 1st sess., 62nd general assembly, 2014, c. 2, SNS 2014, http://bit.ly/2L8tzNE. (The bill has since been passed: https://nslegislature.ca/legc/bills/62nd_1st/3rd_read/b037.htm)
4. "Capital Health Threatens Legal Action If Nurses Resign," *CBC News*, March 20, 2014, http://bit.ly/2ZdoeOT.
5. "Essential Services Bill a Game Changer for Labour Relations," *CBC News*, April 4, 2014, http://bit.ly/2L0fkKB.
6. Eric Boutilier, "Truro Educator: Teachers Tentative Deal a Step Backwards," *The Chronicle Herald*, November 24, 2015.
7. "NSTU Negotiator Urges Teachers to Approve Deal," *The Chronicle Herald*, November 25, 2015.
8. "Tentative Deal Has Ex-NSTU Presidents Critical of Province, Union Leaders," *The Chronicle Herald*, November 27, 2015.
9. Paul McCormick, *Conflict and Collegiality: The Nova Scotia Teachers Union, 1984–2012* (Halifax: Nova Scotia Teachers Union, 2012).
10. Nova Scotia Teachers Union (NSTU), *The Teacher* 55, no. 1 (2016), www.nstu.ca/data/Tmp/TTSept2016rev.pdf.
11. Graham Steele, "Stephen McNeil Triumphs in Labour Negotiations, Says Graham Steele," *CBC News*, November 15, 2015, http://bit.ly/33QycUX.
12. Jennifer Grudic, "Nova Scotia Teachers Reject Second Tentative Agreement," *Global News*, October 4, 2016, globalnews.ca/news/2983038/nova-scotia-teachers-vote-to-reject-tentative-agreement/.
13. Cassie Williams, "Teachers in Nova Scotia to Start Work-to-Rule Job Action Dec. 5," *CBC News*, November 28 2016, http://bit.ly/30oGBwE.
14. Canadian Press, "Nova Scotia to Close All Schools Because Student Safety Can't Be Ensured after Teachers Take Job Action," *National Post*, December 3, 2016, http://bit.ly/30sDhAC.

15. Heide Pearson, "Nova Scotia Teachers Express Frustration with #ReadyToTeach Hashtag on Twitter," *Global News*, December 5, 2016, http://bit.ly/2ZaIkcC.
16. Heide Pearson, "Nova Scotia Schools to Reopen Tuesday, Work-to-Rule Still in Place," *Global News*, December 5, 2016, globalnews.ca/news/3107007/nova-scotia-schools-to-reopen-tuesday/.
17. Jean Laroche, "Taxpayers' Dollars Helped Send Teachers to Hawaii during Work-to-Rule," *CBC News*, January 12, 2017, http://bit.ly/2NvwZgd.
18. The Canadian Press, "Ministers Questions Nova Scotia Teachers' Training Trips during Work-to-Rule," *The Chronicle Herald*, January 12, 2017.
19. Natasha Pace, "Details of NS Teachers' Tentative Agreement Raise Concerns," *Global News*, January 25, 2017, http://bit.ly/2NvV4mK.
20. "Lack of Resources and Supports for Students among Key Factors behind Increased Rates of Violence Towards Teachers," Canadian Teachers' Federation, July 8, 2018, https://bit.ly/349TvzL.
21. Jean Laroche, "Nova Scotia's Teachers to Return to Work-to-Rule on Monday, Says Union," *CBC News*, January 27, 2017, http://bit.ly/2ZuKS4J.
22. Heide Pearson and David Squires, "Bill 75, Legislating a Contract on Nova Scotia's Teachers Becomes Law," *Global News*, February 21, 2017, http://bit.ly/2HkjADH.
23. Darren Calabrese, "Nova Scotia Premier Stephen McNeil Drops Writ for May 30 Election," *Globe and Mail*, April 30, 2017, https://tgam.ca/2YCrXC8
24. Brett Bundale, "N.S. Voter Turnout Slumps to All-Time Low as Less than 54 Per Cent Vote," *CTV News*, May 31, 2017, http://bit.ly/2KPoWcn.

Chapter 9

1. Wikipedia, s.v. "Zach Churchill," last modified April 5, 2018, en.wikipedia.org/wiki/Zach_Churchill.
2. James Faulkner, "Review of Public School Administration Ordered in Nova Scotia," *iHeartradio.com*, October 11, 2017, http://bit.ly/2HkG8nM.

3. Canadian Press, "Nova Scotia Hires Ontario Consultant to Examine Governance of School System," *National Post*, October 11, 2017, http://bit.ly/33QSnC1.
4. Avis Glaze: avisglaze.ca
5. Jean Laroche, "Just-Hired Consultant Has Weeks to Review Education Administration," *CBC News*, October 11, 2017, http://bit.ly/2KPTSsQ.
6. Ibid.
7. Avis Glaze, *Raise the Bar: A Coherent and Responsive Education Administrative System for Nova Scotia* (Halifax: Department of Education and Early Childhood Development, 2018), www.ednet.ns.ca/sites/default/files/docs/raisethebar-en.pdf.
8. Ibid.
9. Ibid., 23.
10. Ibid., 20.
11. "NS Liberal Party Members Vote to Do Away with English Language School Boards," *CKBW*, June 23, 2016, http://bit.ly/2Zb7l7a.
12. Paul W. Bennett, "School Boards Under Fire," AIMS, August 4, 2010, www.aims.ca/in-the-media/school-boards-under-fire/.
13. Diane Ravitch, *Reign of error: The Hoax of the Privatization Movement and the Danger to America's Public Schools* (New York, NY: Knopf, 2014), 280.
14. Glaze, *Raise the Bar*, 33.
15. Ibid., 34.
16. Ibid., 34.
17. Ibid., 36.
18. Department of Education and Early Childhood Development, "Response to the Glaze Report," January 24, 2018, novascotia.ca/news/release/?id=20180124004.
19. "2018 Congress," Canadian School Boards Association, 2018, cdnsba.org/2018-congress.
20. Alexander Quon, "Black Educators Feel Left Behind as N.S. Government Moves Ahead with Glaze Report," *Global News*, February 14, 2018, http://bit.ly/2KPVgf2.
21. Alison Taylor, "'Re-culturing' Students and Selling Futures:

School-to-Work Policy in Ontario," *Journal of Education and Work* 18, no. 3 (2005), 321–340.
22. Glaze, *Raise the Bar*, 33.
23. Canadian Press, "Nova Scotia's Education Reform Bill to Be Introduced Thursday: Premier," *Global News*, February 28, 2018, http://bitly/,2KPG3L5.
24. Caroline Alphonso "Nova Scotia Teachers Vote for Illegal Strike Action That Could Affect 118,000 Students," *Globe and Mail*, February 21, 2018, https://tgam.ca/2MxsrWC.
25. Michael Gorman, "Nova Scotia Teachers Union Says Government 'Has Done Enough' to Avoid Strike," *CBC News*, March 1, 2018, http://bit.ly/31ZJ2Gu.

Chapter 10

1. "Atlantic Institute for Market Studies," Canada Revenue Agency, last modified October 24, 2018, http://bit.ly/2UamwIf.
2. "2018 Registered charity information return for Fraser Institute Foundation," Canada Revenue Agency, reporting period December 31, 2018, https://apps.cra-arc.gc.ca/ebci/hacc/srch/pub/dsplyBscSrch.
3. The Fraser Institute, accessed December 2019, https://www.fraserinstitute.org/.
4. Globe Newswire, "Fraser Institute News Release: AIMS Merges With The Fraser Institute To Create Canada's Largest Independent Public Policy Think-Tank," *The Canadian Business Journal*, November 20, 2019, http://bit.ly/2rLpPf3Index.

Index

Bennett, Paul W., 8, 89, 90–91, 94, 102, 137, 141, 158
blitzkrieg, 149–150, 144–145
Boutilier, Eric, 122

Casey, Karen, 93, 105, 127, 128
Churchill, Zach, 45, 136, 138

Dexter, Darrell, 58, 118, 133
Doucet, Liette, 125, 151

Education Act, 121, 149

Freedman, Joe, 80
Friedman, Milton, 24–25, 33, 73, 75, 82

Glaze report, (see also: *Raise the Bar*), 136–150, 160

Hamm, John, 51–52
Hargreaves, Andy, 43, 47, 67
Harris, Mike, 53, 147
Hayek, Friedrich, 16, 18, 21, 24, 40, 82, 84, 88, 112, 118, 154, 155–156
Hill, Kyle, 106, 107
Horizons, 50, 51, 60, 138
Hudson, Karen, 146

Manley, John, 98, 102
McMahon, Fred, 71, 80

McNeil, Stephen, 72, 105, 118–119, 123, 124, 128, 132, 133, 134, 136
Mitchell, Karen, 94
Morse, Shelley, 95, 125
Murphy, Bob, 88, 89

No Child Left Behind, 32–33, 60, 74

Olsen, Carole, 59, 61

Pink, Ron, 120, 125
Public Service Sustainability Act, 124

Raise the Bar, 60, 138
Ravitch, Diane, 9, 74, 142
Risley, John, 71–72, 79
Rogers, Pamela, 49, 50, 51, 56, 58, 60, 61, 63, 68

Sahlberg, Pasi, 9, 38, 40, 41, 48
Savage, John, 50, 123
Steele, Graham, 105, 123

Teachers' Professional Agreement and Classroom Improvements Act, 10–11, 127–128, 132

The Education Reform Act, 150–151

Zwaagstra, Michael, 81, 158

MARQUIS

Québec, Canada